JAMES DICKEY

Modern Critical Views

These and other titles in preparation

Modern Critical Views

JAMES DICKEY

Edited and with an introduction by
Harold Bloom
Sterling Professor of the Humanities
Yale University

CHELSEA HOUSE PUBLISHERS ◇ 1987
New York ◇ New Haven ◇ Philadelphia

© 1987 by Chelsea House Publishers,
a division of Chelsea House Educational Communications, Inc.,
95 Madison Avenue, New York, NY 10016
345 Whitney Avenue, New Haven, CT 06511
5014 West Chester Pike, Edgemont, PA 19028

Introduction © 1987 by Harold Bloom

Printed and bound in the United States of America

∞ The paper used in this publication meets the minimum
requirements of the American National Standard for
Permanence of Paper for Printed Library Materials,
Z39.48-1984.

Library of Congress Cataloging-in-Publication Data

James Dickey.

(Modern critical views)
Includes index.
Summary: A collection of nine critical essays on
the work of James Dickey, arranged in chronological
order of original publication.
1. Dickey, James—Criticism and interpretation.
[1. Dickey, James—Criticism and interpretation.
2. American literature—History and criticism]
I. Bloom, Harold. II. Series.
PS3554.I32Z74 1987   811'.54   86–34321
ISBN 1–55546–272–3 (alk. paper)

Contents

Editor's Note

This book brings together the best criticism available upon the work of James Dickey. The critical essays are reprinted in the chronological order of their original publication. I am grateful to Neil Arditi for his assistance in researching this volume.

My introduction considers the Dickey of what he calls *The Early Motion: Into the Stone, Drowning With Others,* and *Helmets,* with particular emphasis upon "The Other," "Drowning With Others," "The Heaven of Animals," "Approaching Prayer," and "Drinking from a Helmet."

Laurence Lieberman begins the chronological sequence of criticism with an essay-review of *Falling,* which he judges as having achieved a kind of transcendence. The poet Richard Howard gives us an early overview of Dickey, with a memorable and prophetic conclusion: "No poetry of our time is so determined upon exaltation, no poetry of our time is so exposed to debasement."

In a formal study of Dickey's metric, Paul Ramsey praises "The Owl King" as the poet's best longer work, and rejects "Falling" and "May Day Sermon" as being inhumane and formless. The novelist Joyce Carol Oates studies Dickey as an instance of savagery becoming an ideal in an inevitably faithless society. Our foremost living poet (and Laureate), Robert Penn Warren, reviews *The Zodiac* and salutes it as a paean to the powers and ambitions of poetry.

Dickey's one published novel, *Deliverance,* is read by Linda Wagner as Dickey's best realization of his personal mythmaking, his male vision of initiation through ritual. Neal Bowers centers upon Dickey's advertisements for himself (and for poetry), while Nelson Hathcock offers a full reading of "The Heaven of Animals." In this volume's final essay, the poet James Applewhite offers some luminous reflections upon Dickey's *Puella,* the meditations of a young girl growing up into a woman, a strange revision on the part of this most masculine of all poets.

Introduction

I first read James Dickey's early poem, "The Other," some twenty years ago. Having admired his recently published book, *Drowning With Others,* I went back to his first book, *Into the Stone,* at the recommendation of a close friend, the poet Alvin Feinman. Though very moved by several of the earlier poems, I was affected most strongly by the one called "The Other." It has taken me twenty years to understand why the poem still will not let me go, and so I begin with it here. I don't think of Dickey as a poet primarily of otherness, but rather as a heroic celebrator of what Emerson called "the great and crescive self," indeed of the American self proper, which demands victory and disdains even great defeats. Dickey, as I read him, is like what Vico called the Magic Formalists or Blake named the Giant Forms. He is a throwback to those mythic hypotheses out of which strong poetry first broke forth, the bards of divination whose heroic vitalism demanded a literal immortality for themselves as poets. But even a Magic Formalist learns that he is at best a mortal god.

The pain of that learning is the central story of Dickey's poetry, and I choose to evade that pain here in order to emphasize Dickey's counter-song of otherness. Since I will take him scarcely into his middle years, I will be ignoring all of his most ambitious poetry, "the later motion," as he has called it. Though his work from 1965 to the present clearly is more problematic than the poems I will discuss, its achievement quite possibly is of a higher order. But it is too soon to prophesy Dickey's final stature, and criticism must discourse on what it loves before it broods upon the limits of the canonical. What I know and love best, so far, in Dickey's poetry is "the early motion," and the counter-song of otherness in that motion moves me most. I have circled back to that poem, "The Other," and turn to it now to locate an origin of Dickey's quest as a poet.

That origin is guilt, and guilt ostensibly of being a substitute or replacement for a brother dead before one was born. Freud, I think, would

1

have judged such guilt to be a screen memory, and I am Freudian enough to look or surmise elsewhere for the source of guilt in the poems of *Into the Stone*. From the beginning of his poetic career, Dickey was a poet of Sublime longings, and those who court the Sublime are particularly subject to changeling fantasies. The poem he titled "The Other" is manifestly Yeatsian, whether directly or through the mediation of Roethke, but the argument already is Dickey's own, and in all respects it is the meter-making argument, and not the derived diction and metric, that gives this poem its great distinction. Indeed Dickey, an instinctive Emersonian from the start, despite his Southern heritage, literalizes Emerson's trope of a meter-making argument by the extraordinary device of packing the seventy-seven lines of this lyrical reverie into what has always felt to me like a single sentence. How could there be a second sentence in a poem that identifies itself so completely with the changeling's will to be the other, when the other ultimately is the god Apollo?

Somewhere, Dickey identified his triad of literary heroes as the unlikely combination of Keats, Malcolm Lowry, and James Agee, presumably associated because of their early or relatively early deaths, and because of their shared intensity of belief in what could be called the salvation history of the literary art. But Dickey is very much a poet of Sensibility, in the mode that Frye once defined as *the* Age of Sensibility, the mode of Christopher Smart and of William Collins, among other doomed poets whose threshold stance destroyed them upon the verge of High Romanticism. The Keats who moves Dickey most, the Keats of the letters, is the culmination of the major theme of the poets of Sensibility, the theme that, following Collins, I have called the Incarnation of the Poetical Character. Lowry and Agee, though I don't recall Dickey mentioning this, were curiously allied as verse writers by the overwhelming influence that Hart Crane exerted upon both of them. Dickey seems to prefer Crane's letters to his poems, which oddly parallels his preference of Keats's letters. But Keats and Crane, like Lowry and Agee in their verse, represent fully in their poems the Incarnation of the Poetical Character, where the poet, in the guise of a young man, is reborn as the young god of the sun. That is clearly the genre of Dickey's "The Other," but the clarity is shadowed by Dickey's early guilt concerning what the poem accurately names as "my lust of self."

What self can that be except the magic and occult self, ontological rather than empirical, and in Yeatsian or Whitmanian terms, self rather than soul? The guilt that shadows Dickey's marvelous seventy-seven-line utterance is the guilt induced by what Freud came to call the above-I or the over-I (the superego), a rather more daunting though no less fictive entity than Emerson's Oversoul. Emerson had the shrewdest of eyes for anxiety, but Freud's eye, as Wallace Stevens once wrote, was the microscope of potency. The guilt of family betrayal must ensue from the changeling fantasy of the family romance, and for Freud (as for Kenneth Burke), all romance is family romance. But the family romance of the poet *as* poet tends to depart from the domain of the merely biographical family. Dickey's assertion of self as person was the desire to rise from the "strength-haunted body" of a "rack-ribbed child" to the Herculean figure he has been since, a titanic form among contemporary poets. But since poems can attempt the truth only through fictions or tropes, the poem of "The Other" is compelled to treat the child's aspiration as the drive towards becoming Apollo, poetry itself. The youthful Henry James, reviewing *Drum-Taps,* scorned Whitman as an essentially prosaic temperament trying to lift itself by muscular exertion into poetry. The elderly Henry James, weeping over the great *Lilacs* elegy, scorned his own youthful review; but, properly modified, it can give us a critical trope for reading Dickey: an essentially poetic temperament lifting itself by muscular exertion into poetry.

Dickey's most curious characteristic, from "The Other" through *Puella,* is his involuntary but striking dualism, curious because so heroic a vitalist ought not to exemplify (as he does) so Pauline and Cartesian a mind-body split, or even so prevalent a sense of what Stevens termed the dumbfoundering abyss between ourselves and the object. What the poem surprisingly shows for and to Dickey is that his own body becomes his brother, or Apollo, or "the other." If the body is the divine other, then pathos becomes both sublime and grotesque, because the body must change, and the final form of that change is death. "The Other" is almost the first of Dickey's poems, and in some ways he has never surpassed it, not because he has failed to develop, but because it is unsurpassable. The whole of Dickey is in it already, as the whole of Shelley is in *Alastor,* or the whole of Yeats is in *The Wanderings of Oisin.* I repeat that this does not mean that Dickey simply has unfolded; so restless and reckless an experimentalist is outrageously metamorphic. But all his changes quest hopelessly for a disjunctiveness his temperament refuses to allow him. The "holes" that space out the poems of his major phase never represent discursive gaps or even crossings from one kind of figuration to another. Instead, they impressively mark or punctuate the exquisite desperation of the will to live, the lust of self that is not to be railed at, because it does represent what Keats called "a sickness not ignoble": the sickness unto death of heroic poetry.

"The Other," like so much of Dickey's best work, is very clearly a Southern American poem, and yet its Incarnation of the Poetical Character is necessarily universal in its imagery and argument. This is the universal purchased at the high cost of what was to be a permanent guilt, the guilt of a poet who as poet greatly desired *not* to be egocentric, despite the demands of the mythology that found him from the start. Those demands are felt even in the opening movement of "The Other":

> Holding onto myself by the hand,
> I change places into the spirit
> I had as a rack-ribbed child,
> And walk slowly out through my mind
> To the wood, as into a falling fire
> Where I turned from that strength-haunted body
> Half-way to bronze, as I wished to.

Dickey's natural religion always has been Mithraism, the traditional faith of soldiers, and certainly the most masculine and fierce of all Western beliefs. Despite the Persian origins of Mithra, Rome assimilated him to Apollo, and Dickey's major alteration is to make the Incarnation of the Poetical Character into a Mithraic ritual. The "bronze" of this first stanza will be revealed, later in the poem, as both the statue of Apollo and the body of the sacrificial bull slain by Mithra. As the boy Dickey slings up the too-heavy ax-head, he prays

> To another, unlike me, beside me:
> To a brother or king-sized shadow
> Who looked at me, burned, and believed me:
> Who believed I would rise like Apollo
>
> With armor-cast shoulders upon me:
> Whose voice, whistling back through my teeth,
> Counted strokes with the hiss of a serpent.
> Where the sun through the bright wood drove
> Him, mute, and floating strangely, to the ground,
> He led me into his house, and sat
> Upright, with a face I could never imagine,
>
> With a great harp leant on his shoulder,
> And began in deep handfuls to play it.

"Burned" is the crucial trope here, since the brother, as god of the sun, leads only into the heat and light that is the house of the sun. The oracular hiss is Pythian, though the voice truly becomes Dickey's own. What Dickey, *in the poem,* develops most brilliantly is the figure of downward movement, which is introduced in the second stanza as the combined fall of sweat and leaves, and further invoked in the fall of light. Later in the poem, music falls, followed in the final line by the casting down of foliage. All these fallings substitute for the hidden ritual in which the bull's blood falls upon the Mithraic adept, the warrior in the act of becoming Apollo:

> My brother rose beside me from the earth,
>
> With the wing-bone of music on his back
> Trembling strongly with heartfelt gold,
> And ascended like a bird into the tree,
> And music fell in a comb, as I stood
> In a bull's heavy, bronze-bodied shape
> As it mixed with a god's, on the ground,
> And leaned on the helve of the ax.

The "great, dead tree" of the poem's second stanza might be called Dickey's first major fiction of duration, the origin of his quarrel with time. Being Dickey's, it is the liveliest of dead trees, yet it cannot propitiate this poet's poignant longing for a literal immortality:

> Now, owing my arms to the dead
> Tree, and the leaf-loosing, mortal wood,
> Still hearing that music amaze me,
> I walk through the time-stricken forest,
> And wish another body for my life,
> Knowing that none is given
> By the giant, unusable tree
>
> And the leaf-shapen lightning of sun,
> And rail at my lust of self
> With an effort like chopping through root-stocks:
> Yet the light, looming brother but more
> Brightly above me is blazing,
> In that music come down from the branches
> In utter, unseasonable glory,
>
> Telling nothing but how I made
> By hand, a creature to keep me dying
> Years longer, and coming to sing in the wood
> Of what love still might give,
> Could I turn wholly mortal in my mind,

> My body-building angel give me rest,
> This tree cast down its foliage with the years.

"This tree" is at last Dickey himself as fiction of duration, the poet become his own poem, indeed "made / By hand," and so a house made by hands, a mortal body. When desire can turn monistic, for Dickey, it can become only a mortal turn, a trope knowing it is only trope. The other is divine, but only as Apollo or Mithra was divine, rather than as Jesus or Jehovah. A poem "about" a body-building child has transformed itself into the Sublime, into the body-building angel who has never since given Dickey any rest.

Retrospectively, I suppose that the poem "The Other" first moved me because so few American poems of twenty years ago had anything like Dickey's remarkable ability to be so humanly direct and yet so trustingly given to the potential of figurative language. The Dickey of the early motion seemed to have found his way back, almost effortlessly, to the secrets of poetry. I remember that the first poem by Dickey that I read was the title poem of *Drowning With Others,* a title that is itself an unforgettable trope, worthy of Emily Dickinson's apprehension that an acute consciousness, even when aware of neighbors and the sun, of other selves and outward nature, still died quite alone, except for its own identity, a totemic single hound. What is Sublime in the self finally is capable only of "drowning with others," but that is only part of what is central in what remains one of Dickey's most singular and enduring poems.

If I remember aright, Dickey himself doesn't much like this poem, and thinks it obscure rather than strong. Indeed, I recall his insistence that he wrote the poem only so as to give status to his book's title. His account of the poem's referential aspect was strangely literal, but I think this is one of his poems that sneaked by him, as it were:

> There are moments a man turns from us
> Whom we have all known until now.
> Upgathered, we watch him grow,
> Unshipping his shoulder bones
>
> Like human, everyday wings
> That he has not ever used,
> Releasing his hair from his brain,
> A kingfisher's crest, confused
>
> By the God-tilted light of Heaven.
> His deep, window-watching smile

Comes closely upon us in waves,
And spreads, and now we are

At last within it, dancing.
Slowly we turn and shine
Upon what is holding us,
As under our feet he soars,

Struck dumb as the angel of Eden,
In wide, eye-opening rings.
Yet the hand on my shoulder fears
To feel my own wingblades spring,

To feel me sink slowly away
In my hair turned loose like a thought
Of a fisherbird dying in flight.
If I opened my arms, I could hear

Every shell in the sea find the word
It has tried to put into my mouth.
Broad flight would become of my dancing,
And I would obsess the whole sea,

But I keep rising and singing
With my last breath. Upon my back,
With his hand on my unborn wing,
A man rests easy as sunlight

Who has kept himself free of the forms
Of the deaf, down-soaring dead,
And me laid out and alive
For nothing at all, in his arms.

I read this as another lyric of poetic incarnation, a rather less willing
assumption of the divine other, perhaps even a defense against the Orphic
predicament, but still a revision of the poem "The Other." Indeed, I wonder
if one way of characterizing Dickey's obsessive strength as a poet is to say
that he cannot stop rewriting that essential early poem. For the man who
turns from us in the opening line of "Drowning With Others" is the Orphic
Dickey, poet and divine other. Like the rich-haired youth of Collins, or
Coleridge's youth with flashing eyes and floating hair, or Stevens's figure of
the youth as virile poet in "Mrs. Alfred Uruguay," this other Dickey has hair
released into "a kingfisher's crest, confused / By the God-tilted light of
Heaven." Apollo is reborn again, but as Orphic drowning man, fit version

of the poet of Sensibility in America, be he Hart Crane or Roethke or Agee or Dickey. But if the man turning from us in this poem is Dickey in the act of Sublime apotheosis, then whoever is that "I" rather desperately chanting this hieratic spell? Perhaps that is why Dickey as commentator judged this grand lyric too obscure, despite its palpable strength.

Our poet is weird in the true sense, one of the Fates (as Richard Howard, lexicographer among bards, might remind us), and his natural mode is the uncanny. What he has done here may be obscure to his spectral self, but his magic or occult self gathers his spectral self, until even that "I" keeps "rising and singing / With my last breath." And so truly neither self dies, or can die, in this soaring lyric of divination. Perhaps there is a touch, not indeliberate, of Dylan Thomas in the metric here, and even allusive overtones of Thomas at moments in the diction. That resemblance may even be a hidden cause of Dickey's distaste for his poem, but I remark upon it to note the difference between the poets, rather than their shared qualities. On mortality, the warrior Dickey cannot deceive himself, but a poet whose totem seems to be the albatross does not fear death by water. Few lines are as characteristic of Dickey as "And I would obsess the whole sea."

I take it that "drowning with others" is a trope for "winging with others," and that the dominant image here is flight, and not going under. Flight of course is Freud's true trope for repression, and an Orphic sensibility never ceases to forget, involuntarily but on purpose, that its vocation is mortal godhood, or not dying *as a poet*. Drowning with others, then, as a trope, must mean something like dying only as the immortal precursor dies or writing poems that men will not let die. Though its scale is small, this is Dickey's *Lycidas*, even as *The Zodiac* will be his cosmological elegy for the self. The child building up a Mithra-like body is still here in this poem, but he is here more reluctantly, caught up in the moments of discovering that a too-closely-shared immortality becomes mortality again, the stronger the sharing is known.

Dickey, being one of our authentic avatars of the American Sublime, exemplifies its two grand stigmata: not to feel free unless he is alone, and finally to know that what is oldest in him is no part of the Creation. After two poems wrestling with otherness, I need to restore his sense of solitude, his Emersonian self-reliance, and the great poem for this in his early motion is "In the Mountain Tent," which appropriately concludes the book *Drowning With Others*. I remember that Dickey contrasts this with the more famous "The Heaven of Animals," a lovely poem, but not one with the power of this meditation:

I am hearing the shape of the rain
Take the shape of the tent and believe it,
Laying down all around where I lie
A profound, unspeakable law.
I obey, and am free-falling slowly

Through the thought-out leaves of the wood
Into the minds of animals.
I am there in the shining of water
Like dark, like light, out of Heaven.

I am there like the dead, or the beast
Itself, which thinks of a poem—
Green, plausible, living, and holy—
And cannot speak, but hears,
Called forth from the waiting of things,

A vast, proper, reinforced crying
With the sifted, harmonious pause,
The sustained intake of all breath
Before the first word of the Bible.

At midnight water dawns
Upon the held skulls of the foxes
And weasels and touseled hares
On the eastern side of the mountain.
Their light is the image I make

As I wait as if recently killed,
Receptive, fragile, half-smiling,
My brow watermarked with the mark
On the wing of a moth

And the tent taking shape on my body
Like ill-fitting, Heavenly clothes.
From holes in the ground comes my voice
In the God-silenced tongue of the beasts.
"I shall rise from the dead," I am saying.

Whether a Christian or not, this speaker appears to entertain a belief in the resurrection of the body. Even in this solitude of spirit, the uncanny in Dickey, his *daimon,* enters with the poem's implicit question: Whose body, mine or that of the other? Is it every man who shall rise in the body, or is it not a more Gnostic persuasion that is at work here? The Gnostic lives already in the resurrected body, which is the body of a Primal Man who preceded the Creation. What a Gnostic called the Pleroma, the Fullness, Dickey calls beautifully "the waiting of things." The dead, the animals, and Dickey as the poem's speaker, all hear together the Gnostic Call, a vast crying out of the waiting of things. Without knowing any esoteric Gnosticism, Dickey by poetic intuition arrives at the trope of the Kabbalistic holding in of the divine breath that precedes the rupture of Creation. What Dickey celebrates therefore is "The sustained intake of all breath / Before the first word of the Bible." That word in Hebrew is *Beresit,* and so the vision of this poem is set before the Beginning. At midnight, not at dawn, and so only in the light of a rain image reflected from the beasts, Dickey speaks forth for the beasts, who have been silenced by the Demiurge called God by Genesis. In Dickey's own interpretation, the man experiences both a kinship with the beasts and a fundamental difference, since he alone will rise from the dead. But I think the poet is stronger than the poet-as-interpreter here. To rise from the dead, in this poem's context, is merely to be one's own magical or pneumatic self, a self that precedes the first word of the Bible.

It isn't very startling to see and say that Dickey, as poet, is not a Christian poet, but rather an Emersonian, an American Orphic and Gnostic. This is only to repeat Richard Howard's fine wordplay upon what could be called the Native Strain in our literature. What startles me, a little, is to see and say just how doctrinal, even programmatic, Dickey's early Orphism now seems. The Orphism has persisted, emerging with tumultuous force in the superbly mad female preacher of Dickey's "May Day Sermon," which I recommend we all read directly after each time we read Jonathan Edwards's rather contrary sermon, "Sinners in the Hands of an Angry God." Rhetorically, though, that is a very different Dickey than the poet of *The Early Motion,* whose Orphism perhaps is the more persuasive for being almost overheard, rather than so emphatically heard.

I turn my charting of the early motion to Dickey's next book, *Helmets,* which so far may be his most distinguished single volume, a judgment in which I would neither want nor expect him to concur. "Helmet," as a word, ultimately goes back to an Indo-European root that means both "to cover and conceal," but also "to save," which explains why "helm" and "helmet" are related to those two antithetical primal names, Hell and Valhalla. Dickey's book, of course, knows all this, Dickey being a preternaturally implicit knower, both as a poet and as a warrior—or, combining both modes, as an archer and hunter. Had I time and space, I would want to comment on every poem in *Helmets,* but I will confine myself to its two most ambitious meditations, "Approaching Prayer" and the final "Drinking from a Helmet." Certain thematic and agonistic strains that I have glanced at already can be said not to culminate but to achieve definitive expression in these major poems. I qualify my statement because what is most problematic about Dickey's poetry is that nothing ever is allowed to culminate, not even in *The Zodiac,* or "Falling," or "May Day Sermon." So obsessive a poet generally would not remain also so tentative, but Dickey's is a cunning imagination, metamorphic enough to evade its exegetes.

As a critic himself obsessed with the issue of belatedness, I am particularly impressed by the originality of "Approaching Prayer," which Dickey rightly called "the most complicated and far-fetched poem I've written." I should add that Dickey said that some fifteen years ago, but it is good enough for me that his observation was true up to then. The far-fetcher was the good, rough English term that the Elizabethan rhetorician Puttenham used to translate the ancient trope called metalepsis or transumption, and "Approaching Prayer" is certainly an instance of the kind of poem that I have learned to call transumptive. Such a poem swallows up an ever-early freshness as its own, and spits out all sense of belatedness, as belonging only to others. "Approaching Prayer" is at moments Yeatsian in its stance and diction, but what overwhelmingly matters most in it can only be called "originality." I know no poem remotely like it. If it shares a magic vitalism with Yeats and D. H. Lawrence, its curious kind of wordless, almost undirected prayer has nothing Yeatsian or Lawrentian in its vision. And it is less like Dickey's true precursor, Roethke, than it is like Robert Penn Warren's masterful "Red-Tailed Hawk and Pyre of Youth," which, however, was written long after it and perhaps may even owe something to it.

Originality in poetry, despite Northrop Frye's eloquent assertions, has little to do with the renewal of an archetype. Instead, it has to do with what I would call a struggle against facticity, where "facticity" means being so incarcerated by an author, a tradition, or a mode that neither author nor reader is aware of the incarceration. Dickey calls his poem "Approaching Prayer," but as his revisionist or critic, I will retitle it "Approaching Poetry" or even "Approaching Otherness." I grant that Dickey has said, "In this poem I tried to imagine how a rather prosaic person would prepare himself for the miraculous event which will be the prayer he's going to try to pray," but surely that "rather prosaic person" is a transparent enough defense for the not exactly prosaic Dickey. No one has ever stood in Dickey's presence and felt that he was encountering prose. The poem's speaker is "inside the hair *helmet*" (my emphasis), and this helmet too both conceals and saves. At the poem's visionary center, the boar's voice, speaking through the helmet, gives us the essential trope as he describes his murder by the archer: *"The sound from his fingers, / Like a plucked word, quickly pierces / Me again."* The bow, then, is poetic language, and each figuration is a wounding arrow. Who then is slaying whom?

Like any strong poet, Dickey puts on the body of his dead father, for him, let us say, the composite precursor Yeats/Roethke. Shall we say that the strong poet, in Dickey's savage version, reverses the fate of Adonis, and slays the boar of facticity? I hear the accent of another reversal, when Dickey writes:

> My father's sweater
> Swarms over me in the dark.
> I see nothing, but for a second
>
> Something goes through me
> Like an accident, a negligent glance.

Emerson, in his famous epiphany of transmutation into a Transparent Eyeball, chanted: "I am nothing; I see all; the currents of the Universal Being circulate through me; I am part or particle of God." Dickey's surrogate sees nothing, but for a second is all, since that something going through him, glancingly negligent, accidental, also makes him part or particle of God. Addressing beasts and angels, this not so very prosaic personage speaks both as beast and as angel. But to whom? To part or particle of what is oldest, earliest in him, to the beyond that comes straight down at the point of the acceptable time. But acceptable to whom? The God of the hunt is hardly Yahweh Elohim. Dickey's closing chant salutes the God through the trope of "enough": a violent enough stillness, a brain having enough blood, love enough from the dead father, lift enough from the acuity of slaughter— all enough to slay reason in the name of something being, something that need not be heard, if only "it may have been somehow said." The apocalyptic Lawrence of the last poems and *The Man Who Died,* and the Yeats of the final phase, celebrated and so would have understood that "enough." As an American Orphic, as pilot and as archer, Dickey is less theoretic, more pragmatic, in having known just that "enough."

If I were writing of the later Dickey, the poet of "The Firebombing," "Slave Quarters," "Falling," and *The Zodiac,* then I would invoke Blake's Proverbs of Hell on the dialectics of knowing enough by knowing more than enough. But I am going to conclude where Dickey himself ends *The Early Motion,* with the gracious approach to otherness that characterizes the nineteen fragments that constitute "Drinking from a Helmet." Dickey remarks that the fragments are set between the battlefield and the graveyard, which I suspect is no inaccurate motto for the entire cosmos of what will prove to be the Whole Motion, when we have it all. Though it is a suite of war poems, "Drinking from a Helmet," even in its title, moves toward meaning both of Dickey's major imaginative obsessions: divination through finding the right cover of otherness, and salvation from the body of this death through finding the magic body of the poet.

A survivor climbs out of his foxhole to wait on line at a green water-truck, picking up another's helmet to serve as a drinking vessel. Behind him, the graves registration people are laying out the graveyard for those still fighting. The literal force of this is almost too strong, and conceals the trope of divination, defined by Vico as the process of evasion by which the poet of Magic Formalism achieves godhood—a kind of mortal godhood, but immortality enough. Drinking from a helmet becomes the magic act of substitution, fully introduced in the luminous intensity of fragment VIII:

> At the middle of water
> Bright circles dawned inward and outward
> Like oak rings surviving the tree
> As its soul, or like
> The concentric gold spirit of time.
> I kept trembling forward through something
> Just born of me.

The "something" is prayer, but again in the peculiar sense adumbrated in the poem "Approaching Prayer." Dickey always has been strongest at *invention* (which Dr. Johnson thought the essence of poetry) and his invention is triumphant throughout the subsequent progression of fragments. We apprehend an almost Blakean audacity of pure vision, as the speaker struggles to raise the dead:

> I swayed, as if kissed in the brain.
> Above the shelled palm-stumps I saw
> How the tops of huge trees might be moved
> In a place in my own country
> I never had seen in my life.
> In the closed dazzle of my mouth
> I fought with a word in the water
> To call on the dead to strain
> Their muscles to get up and go there.
> I felt the difference between

> Sweat and tears when they rise,
> Both trying to melt the brow down.

I think one would have to go back to Whitman's *Drum-Taps* to find an American war poem this nobly wrought. Vision moves from Okinawa to rural America, to the place of the slain other whose helmet has served as the vessel of the water of life:

> On even the first day of death
> The dead cannot rise up,
> But their last thought hovers somewhere
> For whoever finds it.
> My uninjured face floated strangely
> In the rings of a bodiless tree.
> Among them, also, a final
> Idea lived, waiting
> As in Ariel's limbed, growing jail.

Ariel, imprisoned by the witch before Prospero's advent, then becomes the spirit of freedom, but not in this poem, where only to "be no more killed" becomes freedom enough. "Not dying wherever you are" is the new mode of otherness, as vision yields to action:

> Enough
> Shining, I picked up my carbine and said.
> I threw my old helmet down
> And put the wet one on.
> Warmed water ran over my face.
> My last thought changed, and I knew
> I inherited one of the dead.

Dickey at last, though only through surrogate or trope, is at once self and other. What was vision becomes domesticated, touchingly American:

> I saw tremendous trees
> That would grow on the sun if they could,
> Towering. I saw a fence
> And two boys facing each other,
> Quietly talking,
> Looking in at the gigantic redwoods,
> The rings in the trunks turning slowly
> To raise up stupendous green.
> They went away, one turning

The wheels of a blue bicycle,
The smaller one curled catercornered
In the handlebar basket.

The dead soldier's last thought is of his older brother, as Dickey's longing always has been for his own older brother, dead before the poet was born. Fragment XVIII, following, is the gentlest pathos in all of Dickey:

I would survive and go there,
Stepping off the train in a helmet
That held a man's last thought,
Which showed him his older brother
Showing him trees.
I would ride through all
California upon two wheels
Until I came to the white
Dirt road where they had been,
Hoping to meet his blond brother,
And to walk with him into the wood
Until we were lost,
Then take off the helmet
And tell him where I had stood,
What poured, what spilled, what swallowed:

That "what" is the magic of substitution, and the final fragment is Whitmanian and unforgettable, being the word of the survivor who suffered and was there:

And tell him I was the man.

The ritual magic of a soldier's survival has been made one with the Incarnation of the Poetical Character. Of all Dickey's poems, it is the one I am persuaded that Walt Whitman would have admired most. Whitman too would have said with Dickey: "I never have been able to disassociate the poem from the poet, and I hope I never will." What Whitman and Dickey alike show is that "the poet" is both an empirical self, and more problematically a real me or me myself, an ontological self, and yet a divine other. Both poets are hermetic and esoteric while making populist gestures. There the resemblance ends, and to pursue it further would be unfair to Dickey or any contemporary; it would have been unfair even for Stevens or for Hart Crane. The Dickey of the later motion is no Whitmanian; if one wants an American analogue, one would have to imagine Theodore Roethke as an astronaut, which defeats imagination. But I end by citing Whitman because his final gestures are the largest contrast I know to James Dickey's ongoing motions in his life's work. Whitman is up ahead of us somewhere; he is perpetually early, warning us: "Will you speak before I am gone? will you prove already too late?" The burden of belatedness is upon us, but if we hurry, we will catch up to him:

> Failing to fetch me at first keep encouraged,
> Missing me one place search another,
> I stop somewhere waiting for you.

Not Dickey; he cannot stop, yet he has taken up part of the burden for us. Whitman is larger, but then no one is larger, and that largeness is a final comfort, like Stevens's "Large Red Man Reading." Dickey speaks only to and for part of us, but that part is or wants to be the survivor; wants no more dying. Words alone, alas, are not certain good, though the young Yeats, like the young Dickey, wanted them to be. But they can help us to make "a creature to keep me dying / Years longer," as Dickey wrote in the poem of "The Other." I conclude by going full circle, by returning to the poem with the tribute that it could prove to contain the whole motion within it. Dickey cannot "turn wholly mortal in [his] mind," and that touch of "utter, unseasonable glory" will be his legacy.

LAURENCE LIEBERMAN

James Dickey: The Deepening of Being

The poetic vision in James Dickey's fifth volume of poems, *Falling,* contains so much joy that it is incapable of self-pity or self-defeat. There is a profound inwardness in the poems, the inner self always celebrating its strange joy in solitude, or pouring outward, overflowing into the world. No matter how much suffering the poet envisions, the sensibility that informs and animates him is joy in the sheer pleasure of being.

The condition of joy works remarkable transformations, in literature as in life, often converting the tragic condition into a saving buoyancy. This power to transform is typical of the best poems in the romantic tradition. It derives from a special conjunction of the intelligence with the poetic imagination. The transforming joy in Yeats's poetry works its way into the antithetical spheres of private and public life. One measure of the greatness of Yeats's achievement is the expansion in the scope of his vision to include, with equal rigor and authority, personal disasters of the self and global catastrophes such as the Irish Revolution and World War I. The joyful vision of Theodore Roethke, the American poet for whom Dickey feels the strongest spiritual affinity, rarely extends into the political arena; instead, it journeys forever inward, probing darker and more perilous recesses of the interior self. The more tragic emotion—suffering, bitterness, despair—art can absorb and transmute into joyousness of being, the healthier it is. Dickey's vision aspires, above all, to that kind of supernal healthiness, but it moves uneasily into larger sociopolitical issues of War and Race. His joyousness is generous to a fault, uncontrollable—thus working to disadvan-

From *The Achievement of James Dickey.* © 1968 by Laurence Lieberman. Scott, Foresman, 1968.

tage in a few of his most ambitious poems. In "The Firebombing" and "Slave Quarters," for example, the moments of ecstasy threaten to overbalance the moments of agony.

In the four volumes prior to *Falling*, Dickey seems to vacillate, as did Yeats, between two spiritual poles: stoicism and romantic passion. The problem of facing death without fear elicits by turns, now one, now the other, as in "The Ice Skin":

> Not knowing whether
> I will break before I can feel,
>
> Before I can give up my powers,
> Or whether the ice light
>
> In my eyes will ever snap off
> Before I die.

The ice light, a heroic "masterly shining," is a dispassionate state, a calm radiance of the spirit learned through a series of existential encounters with "the dying" and the "just born." The prevailing spirit of the poem is the power to endure suffering and meet death quietly, with steadiness and poise—a stoical transcendence over death by intellect.

However, Dickey's vision is far more sustaining when he achieves transcendence over death by passion, intensity of self, deepening of being, as in "The Performance," an early war poem that, with "The Jewel," initiates a sequence of war poetry culminating in a poem of the first importance, "The Firebombing."

In making an assessment of Dickey's war poetry we must ask, Does the sum total of the author's writings on the subject of war move us to respond humanely to the massive political crisis of our generation—that is, to respond with the human, or superhuman, compassion and commitment necessary to redress the wrongs, first, in our individual souls, and last, in the soul of our Age?

In "The Performance," the Japanese executioner will have to carry the scars of Donald Armstrong's death in his soul, since, miraculously, Armstrong's ritual performance has converted the mechanical, inhuman relation between executioner and victim into a personal and inescapably spiritual—an existential—encounter:

> the headsman broke down
> In a blaze of tears, in that light
> Of the thin, long human frame

Upside down in its own strange joy,
And, if some other one had not told him,
Would have cut off the feet

Instead of the head.

The fatally impersonal relation between man and man is a central dilemma of our time, occurring in its ultimate form in war. In "The Firebombing," Dickey conceives the dilemma of impersonality as being insoluble. The protagonist, however hard he tries, cannot connect spiritually with his victims below. Conversely, in "The Performance," the ritual acrobatic stunts create personal being, restore the I-thou, so that even the headsman, though powerless to disobey his superiors and follow his impulse to spare Armstrong's life, finds a kind of spiritual absolution during the killing. Armstrong's acrobatics transform the killing relation between them into a saving relation, a forgiving relation. Both souls are saved.

If many veterans are content to claim the depersonalization of their acts and the beings from which they sprang—in war time—as grounds for absolving themselves of personal responsibility for their crimes, James Dickey is not. Witness his mercilessly uncompromising self-judgment in "The Jewel." Recalling his years as a fighter pilot, not only does he impute personal involvement to his flying missions, but he remembers feeling the sort of joyful fascination for his life in the cockpit that men ordinarily feel for precious gems. He is a passive lover—mated to his plane—who allows himself to be abducted by the overpowering beauty of the machinery, "being the first to give in / To the matched priceless glow of the engines." He sees himself lovingly enclosed in the jewel-cockpit, as in the warmth of a womb. Now, years later, in the warmth of the family tent during a holiday, he recalls the pleasure he received from the enclosure of the plane. The old joy floods into the present, mocking his present security, leaving him feeling, once again, more than ever alone in his soul's late night.

"The Jewel" is one of Dickey's earliest attempts to identify and cope with the residue of guilt left by his role in the war. In the poem, the poet sees himself more as a paroled or pardoned criminal than as a survivor. But can he pardon himself? Does he qualify as a spiritual parolee? "The Jewel" is a predecessor of "The Firebombing" in a way the other war poems are not. In "The Performance" and "Drinking from a Helmet," he allows himself to feel the innocence and compassion of the detached bystander, a stance that conveniently removes the persona from his guilt, so the horror of war may be treated as a subject in itself, apart from whatever moral responsibility he may himself feel for perpetrating evil of his own making or perpetuating evil set in motion by the State.

In "Drinking from a Helmet," a new form—employing short self-contained numbered sections in place of the usual stanza units—facilitates a rapid to-and-fro fluctuation between inner experience and external action. It moves almost effortlessly between controlled hallucination and stark realism, a remarkably apt strategy for a poem that sets out to present extraordinary spiritual events in a setting of extreme dehumanization. Written in a tradition of war poetry, running from Wilfred Owen to Randall Jarrell, in which spiritual uplift in the midst of carnage of battle would be unthinkable, Dickey's poem provides uplift as much because of the soul's depravity as in spite of it.

In the opening sections of "Drinking from a Helmet," the level of awareness of the speaker keeps shifting, refocusing. He is possessed by two beings, recognizably separate early in the poem. Who is speaking, I or ultra-I?

> In the middle of combat, a graveyard
> Was advancing after the troops
>
> .   .   .   .
>
> A green water-truck stalled out.
> I moved up on it, behind
> The hill that cut off the firing.
>
> .   .   .   .
>
> I swayed, as if kissed in the brain.

One being perceives everything with a casual directness, a down-to-earthness necessary to mental self-preservation ("A green water-truck stalled out"); the other registers profound ultra-events ("I swayed, as if kissed in the brain"). The two zigzag, at irregular intervals, through the voice of the speaker, without any noticeable jarring of tone. The voice provides a continuum that can contain both irreducible beings, and gradually the two converge and interpenetrate in the vision of the poem's action:

> I threw my old helmet down
> And put the wet one on.
> Warmed water ran over my face.
> My last thought changed, and I knew
> I inherited one of the dead.

The speaker has imbibed and mystically reincarnated the spirit of the dead soldier in his own living spirit by drinking water from the man's helmet.

In the closing sections, as he envisions a plan to transport the dead man's spirit to his brother's home in California, incredible life bursts into the poem:

> I would survive and go there,
> Stepping off the train in a helmet
> That held a man's last thought
>
> . . . .
>
> I would ride through all
> California upon two wheels
>
> . . . .
>
> Hoping to meet his blond brother,
> And to walk with him into the wood
> Until we were lost,
> Then take off the helmet
> And tell him where I had stood,
> What poured, what spilled, what swallowed:
>
> And tell him I was the man.

The poem creates the illusion, finally, of being a prayer girding the speaker for a move back into life. The poem is like a launching pad to an actual experience; simultaneously, it contains within itself that future experience and opens into the event-to-be. The barrier between poem and lived act is swept away, just as the threshold between the living and dead soldiers was dissolved earlier in the poem.

In "The Firebombing," also, two beings function simultaneously but separately. In "Helmet," the two beings are coincident in time but move in different psychic levels. In "The Firebombing," present being collides with past being. Both seem to be hopelessly blocked, ineligible for entry into the full import of the experience—one lost in time, the other in moral stupor. Will the collision between the two lost selves, in the dream-dance of flight, result in a clarity of mind within which the unified self may seek absolution through a true confrontation with its crimes? This question comprises the central strategy of "The Firebombing."

At the finish, Dickey explicitly admits his failure to achieve his intended end: to assuage the moral guilt for past crimes by experiencing again the events in the imagination. He tried, through the medium—and mediation—of the poem, to feel some of the human horror and shame that his moral conscience tells him he should have felt twenty years before, and thereby to achieve moral expiation through art—the fire in the poem would cleanse the author's soul, purify it, burn away the sense of sin. But he finds, in the most piercingly honest revelation the poem affords, that art itself is an unclean instrument in his hands. The feelings of guilt and horror stirred by the experience of the poem cannot effect catharsis because they are hampered by the remembered sense of beauty and joy felt during the act of murder, "this detachment, / The honored aesthetic evil, / The greatest sense of power in one's life."

Early in the poem, it becomes evident to the reader that the moral jeopardy of the present is just as insuperable as that of the past. Self-purification must occur in the world of the suburban present, but the handicap of present prosperity and excess spreads across the poem in a Whitmanesque catalogue of luxuries that quickly accumulate into an insurmountable obstacle to the self's redemption. There are many self-scalding images that take the speaker part way through the complex initiation ceremonies his redemption requires:

> It [the blazing napalm] consumes them in a hot
> Body-flash, old age or menopause
> Of children, clings and burns.

If such images don't contain seeds of expiation, how can ideas or slogans, or even direct prayer, redeem him?

Dickey finds himself in much the same position as Claudius, who fails in the sincere attempt to repent of the murder of the elder Hamlet because he still possesses the spoils of the crime, queen and kingdom, and knows he is too weak to give them up. Likewise, not only is Dickey still blessed, or cursed, with the luxuries of the American suburban middle class, but he persists in being as "American as I am, and proud of it." Further, Dickey's incapacity "to get down there or see / What really happened" can be attributed to other factors. First, the only way you can know exactly what it feels like to see your own child (or your neighbor's) walk through a door "With its ears crackling off / Like powdery leaves" is to see it actually happen. Second, in writing the poem, Dickey places himself once again in the "blue light" of the "glass treasure-hole," deep in the same "aesthetic contemplation" he felt as he flew over "The *heart* of the fire." His spirit is perplexed by his joy in the act of writing, trapped in the tools of his art.

The poet senses that the experience of the actual firebombing gave birth in his soul to his deepest aesthetic instincts and talents, which he has never before more directly exploited than in the writing of "The Firebombing."

Ironically, the poem seems better even for his having interrupted its flow of experience at the finish to comment on its inevitable failure to achieve its main goal:

> Absolution? Sentence? No matter;
> The thing itself is in that.

Perhaps this is a sort of ironic punishment: the poem gets better as the author backs away from it, refuses to exult over its beauties, insists that the purely human act of salvation from this massive sin is too great a burden for this poem, or indeed any poem, to carry.

How, then, do we account for the success of the poem, not only as art, but as a human (politically human, even) document? How account for the success of a major poem which unconditionally fails to achieve what the author explicitly intended it to achieve? Simply by acknowledging that whatever is not contained in "the thing itself"—the dramatic confrontation between self and its guilt, its crimes, in the action of the poem—cannot be stated parenthetically at the end as an afterthought, a dissipated message. To state it so would be to falsify the poem's central concern and mode of delivery. The writer has attempted the impossible, and he admits it. He is not ready for self-forgiveness yet, because he is not yet able to feel a guilt commensurate with his crimes. Perhaps he never will be ready. These are grave truths, but they are fully realized truths nonetheless, however lacking they may be in the kind of heroism fashionable at peace rallies in the Sixties.

Moreover, if the poem admits its own failure to feel what must be felt, it carries the reader a step closer to having the feelings necessary to spiritual survival, and carries the instrument of language a step closer to meeting the ultimate life-challenge art faces in our time. If we read this poem—and, indeed, all Dickey's best work—with the brain in our eyes, with the intelligence to see what we call a *vision*, we find it to be poetry that constantly sends *us* back from the printed page to the gravest life-challenges.

As a survivor of two wars, Dickey feels spiritually hunted by disinherited beings (pursued by the "downed dead," as in "Pursuit from Under"), who silently accuse him of usurping their birthright to existence, leaving him with intimations of spiritual illegitimacy:

> Out of grief, I was myself
> Conceived, and brought to life
> To replace the incredible child
> . . . .

> *Dead before I was born.*
> ("The String")

In a number of war poems—"The Firebombing" particularly—Dickey feels like a cosmic criminal who, by luck or trickery, has miraculously escaped punishment and walks in freedom while innocent souls rot in purgatorial confinement, serving an eternal sentence for another's, his, crimes. He finds most harrowing the thought that he has been personally responsible for the death of many Japanese women and children, and in some poems he tries desperately to make his peace with the phantoms from death's dream kingdom.

Another source of these psychic misgivings is the stories he was often told by his parents about the brother who was "dead before I was born," stories antedating his war years by long enough to have been buried deeply in his memory, ready to be disinterred years later. The stories became indelibly, if invisibly, stamped on his impressionable young mind, and they haunted his early childhood, when he often felt as if he were possessed by a disembodied alter-self, living "within another's life." This long-forgotten obsession revisits him in his early poems, and he shapes it into a unique personal myth or legend. It is the first in a chain of mystiques that embody Dickey's developing logos of being.

To assuage his inexplicable guilt, the poet seeks devices for the revival of dead beings. In "The String," the dying brother's string-tricks, such as "foot of a crow," are conceived of as the ritual magic that can guarantee his eternal return in living beings. The performance can be imitated by the living and used as a way of entering the dead child's being or of taking his being into oneself. The ritual performance with the string converted the brother's dying into an act of love. But it was purely self-love. There was no hint of the child's reaching out to others—parents or friends—through the string-game. Contrarily, the speaker's performance with the string is a love act that engages the other being deeply. It connects him with the dead brother, and he aspires to use it to connect the living parents to the brother, but fails: "I believe in my father and mother / Finding no hope in these lines."

A comparison between "The String" and the later "Power and Light" can be used to illustrate the remarkable distance Dickey's art has traveled between his first book and *Falling*. In "The String" he connects his own being to the Other, the spirits of the dead, but cannot, or will not, mediate between others as a neutral, but fiercely charged, spiritual conductor, as in "Power and Light":

                    and I feel the wires running
Like the life-force along the limited rafters   and all connections
With poles   with the tarred naked belly-buckled black
Trees I hook to my heels   with the shrill phone calls leaping
Long distance   long distances through my hands   all connections

Even the one
With my wife, turn good

·   ·   ·   ·   ·   ·   ·   ·
                    Never think I don't know my profession
Will lift me: why, all over hell the lights burn in your eyes,
People are calling each other   weeping with a hundred thousand
Volts   making deals   pleading   laughing like fate,
Far off, invulnerable   or with the right word pierced

To the heart
By wires I held, shooting off their ghostly mouths,
In my gloves.

The power lines of this poem exceed the string by the same vast margin as "Power and Light" surpasses "The String" in spiritual intensity.

In "The String," as in most poems in *Into the Stone,* ritual hangs back from the reader in an ephemeral landscape of dream-memory. The reader is enticed by the strangeness of images, and if he feels somehow left outside the speaker's experience—a charmed, but displaced, onlooker—he is persuaded mentally by the ingenuity of the poem's argument:

> My eyes go from me, and down
> Through my bound, spread hands
> To the dead, from the kin of the dead.

In a number of the earlier poems, however, the gap between the reader's life-experience and the poem's drama is too large. In an attempt to bridge the gap, the mind's activity, in the form of willed images or willed ideas, dominates the poem. The reader recoils from the tone of intellectual stridency as the poem's everextended machinery quavers like a house of cards.

In contrast, in many lines of "In the Tree House at Night," a later poem that revives the dead brother's spirit, there *is* something of the lightness of air—one can almost hear inbreathing sounds, a wind-sucking voice:

> The floor and walls wave me slowly

. . . .

In the arm-slender forks of our dwelling

I breathe my live brother's light hair.

It is perhaps no accident that in the early poems we find the inexplicable beginnings of a vision of genesis in air that eventually develops into the fulfilled air-birth of Dickey's most achieved vision, in "Falling." Unlike the play-dwellings of "The String," the hypnotic lyricism of "Tree House" creates a castle in air that takes the reader's heaviness away and converts him into a being afloat, a just-lighter-than-air self. The poem's drama instills the sense of flying, of a soul set free in its body:

When may I fall strangely to earth,

Who am nailed to this branch by a spirit?

In "Tree House," atmospheric elements of scene, setting, time of day—all become dynamically enmeshed in the poem's drama. As in a movie, these elements create the illusion of action taking place *now*. The ritual magic of the poem's movement pulls the reader, irresistibly, into its happening. He is himself one of the actors, sharing the tree house of the poem's ritual flight with "My brothers and I, one dead, / The other asleep from much living, / In mid-air huddled beside me."

In "Tree House," as in the other best poems of the second volume, *Drowning With Others,* Dickey evolves a mode of experiencing a double vision that seems ideally suited to his poetic imagination, thereby anticipating the more complex dualism of later poems like "Drinking from a Helmet" and "Firebombing." Two separate, but interdependent, dramas occur simultaneously in "Tree House." A familiar scene or event is presented directly, and an equally clear and sharp experience of the spirit is envisioned through it. Usually, in the best poems, the two dramas, outer and inner, are nearly evenly balanced. Neither dominates the poem. The poem can be read with equal interest at either level, but it is experienced, ideally, at both.

A lifeguard trying to forgive himself for letting a child drown, two brothers striving to oppose the real world with the fantasy world of their tree house—both are familiar experiences and hence create immediate and intensified human interest, but they become unfamiliar, beautiful, and strange as a unique spiritual experience is filtered through them. The familiar story seems, of necessity, to call up from the inner depths a strangely new spiritual history to explain it. At the same time, the spirit half creates the illusion of being the reflection or mirror image of the story half—the familiar leading, effortlessly, into the unfamiliar, and back again. If the spirit half dominates many of the best early poems, the story half dominates Dickey's best later poems—"The Shark's Parlor," "The Sheep Child," "Falling"—in which the poet is bent on exploring novel, rather than ordinary, experience, to stir up strangely new spiritual overtones, and to extend the resources of his art.

In "Tree House" and "The Lifeguard," a familiar experience is turned inside out. As the poems proceed, the focus of the drama shifts from the outer world of story to the inner world of magic. What begins as a tale of two boys playing house in a tree changes into a mystical vision in which the speaker experiences a transmigration of three beings—his own, his dead brother's, and his sleeping brother's—through the medium of the tree. The state of spirits in flux is expertly dramatized by lines that enter the inexplicable thresholds between brother and brother, alive and dead, asleep and awake:

> I stir
> Within another's life. Whose life?
> Who is dead? Whose presence is living?
>
> . . . .
>
> Can two bodies make up a third?

The lifeguard returns to the scene of his defeat and recounts his failed attempt to save the drowned child's life in details that suggest the pain of self-mutilation:

> And my fingertips turned into stone
> From clutching immovable blackness.

His ritual suffering, in memory, summons the dead child's spirit to his aid. Though he is still "thinking of how I may be / The savior of one / Who has already died in my care," paradoxically, the relation between saver and saved is reversed through the medium of water as the dead child's spirit rises to free the living, helpless man from his guilt.

Both poems awaken the reader to the unexpected realization that a profound spiritual life lies hidden just below the surface of most routine experiences, and that perhaps this inner life of being is inherent in all experience, waiting to be released by the healthy imagination. This inner life erupts with the intensity of hallucination and pervades our being with the strangeness of the supernatural, yet it is, at all times, available to the normal mind. It is a richer totality of being than we are accustomed to enjoying in our daily lives. It seems to be delivered to the conscious self as from an inexhaustible source. At a moment's notice, it can transform grief into boundless joy. It is a state in which each one's being is both alone in a self-contained peace and indissolubly connected, in love, to other beings, living and dead, as in the beautiful closing lines of "Tree House":

> To sing, must I feel the world's light?
> My green, graceful bones fill the air
> With sleeping birds. Alone, alone
> And with them I move gently.
> I move at the heart of the world.

Never again in his poems about children does Dickey achieve such a full expression of the way he perceives the strange beauty—the otherness—of children's fantasy-vision as he does in "The Lifeguard" and "Tree House." Yet in neither of these poems do we find purely a child's vision; rather, they offer a vision inaccessible to children, possible only to a man childlike in his freedom from incapacitating rigidities of mind and in his absolute faith in the saving power of imagination. The lifeguard's vision contains, in addition, the belief that a powerful healing forgiveness dwells in the souls of small children: a forgiveness strong enough to balance a man's guilt for taking the place of the brother "dead before I was born," and a healing power soothing enough to close temporarily the wound sustained by his spirit when he poured fire-death on the children of Japan. The evidence of thematic development strongly suggests that the guilt that is partly assuaged through the persona of the lifeguard is only temporarily forestalled, while the poet gradually fortifies his craft to deal with the larger challenge of a direct encounter, in art, with the events of the war which planted in his heart seeds of guilt that can never be entirely purged or expunged. The searing, insurmountable guilt is presented in raw form in many lines and images in "The Firebombing," and, again, in the final passage of "Slave Quarters," in which the southern white father meditates on the face of his choice possession, an illegitimate mulatto son:

> There is no hatred
> Like love in the eyes
> Of a wholly owned face? When you think of what
> It would be like   what it has been
> What it is to look once a day
> Into an only
> Son's brown, waiting, wholly possessed

Amazing eyes, and not
Acknowledge, but own?

Dickey's imagination is obsessed with a man's responsibility—human and mystical—for the lives of children, especially those entrusted to his care. It is one of the very few themes that have engaged him deeply at each stage of his development, the problem having its own self-defined limits, peculiarity, and obsessive strangeness. Dickey is always at his best when he tackles a subject that entirely engrosses and excites his imagination, such as the most basic challenges to his manhood—befriending, fathering, husbanding.

One of Dickey's most sustaining and pervasive faiths is his absolute belief that the human imagination can save us from anything. No human disaster or tragedy is too large for the imagination to encompass or too crushing for imagination to convert it into lifesavingness. This credo reaches its culmination, and its apotheosis, in the poem "Falling." Who would have guessed that a woman's falling to her death from a plane could be converted by Dickey's imagination into a symbol of fantastic affirmation of life? The thought of his being responsible for the death of a child fills Dickey's heart with extreme terror, a terror that arouses an instantaneous sympathy and recognition in most readers. Every parent harbors a secret voice in his soul repeating over and over—consciously or unconsciously—that if harm or injury comes to his child through his neglect, he'll never forgive himself. That *never* is a powerful and terrifying idea, and Dickey's imagination obstinately refuses to submit to never. Some of his best poems, such as "The Lifeguard" and "The Firebombing," are desperate attempts to forgive himself, spiritually, for what he recognizes to be humanly unforgivable.

The development of Dickey's treatment of the theme of human/animal relations is central to his art. Moreover, since this theme is unhampered by the overwhelming moral guilt of much of the war poetry and the poems about children, it can be used to demonstrate an evolving logos of being.

Dickey's engagement with the animal world was never cultivated simply as equipment for his poetry. He is intent on exploring the animal's dimensions of being. His experience of hunting, like that of soldiering, antedates his career in poetry by many years. As in the war poetry, the passion he feels for hunted animals is so intense that it enables him to put out of his mind the tradition of nature poetry in English—D. H. Lawrence's excepted—and induce a literary amnesia, allowing him the latitude of imagination necessary to do justice to a series of strangely unique human/animal encounters.

The stages of relationship he depicts closely resemble those of a love affair between man and woman, especially in the way the poet's mind explores possibilities—limits—of relationship in search of a truer sense of identity. Dickey's realization of personal identity is always sought through a deep conjunction with the Other, whether the Other happens to take the form of animals, children, man, or woman. Consider, for example, "The Heaven of Animals":

> Here they are. The soft eyes open.
> If they have lived in a wood
> It is a wood.
> If they have lived on plains
> It is grass rolling
> Under their feet forever.
>
> Having no souls, they have come,
> Anyway, beyond their knowing.
> Their instincts wholly bloom
> And they rise.
> The soft eyes open.
>
> To match them, the landscape flowers,
> Outdoing, desperately
> Outdoing what is required:
> The richest wood,
> The deepest field.
>
> For some of these,
> It could not be the place
> It is, without blood.
> These hunt, as they have done,
> But with claws and teeth grown perfect,
>
> More deadly than they can believe.
> They stalk more silently,
> And crouch on the limbs of trees,
> And their descent
> Upon the bright backs of their prey
>
> May take years
> In a sovereign floating of joy.
> And those that are hunted

Know this as their life,
Their reward: to walk

Under such trees in full knowledge
Of what is in glory above them,
And to feel no fear,
But acceptance, compliance.
Fufilling themselves without pain

At the cycle's center,
They tremble, they walk
Under the tree,
They fall, they are torn,
They rise, they walk again.

"The Heaven of Animals" is a classically pure statement. It pictures the animals in an utterly unpeopled landscape that recalls D. H. Lawrence's wistful misanthropic vision in *Women in Love* of a world "all grass and a hare standing up." Dickey conceives of the animals as being ideally beautiful and innocent, incapable of evil. All violence, or bloodshed, is performed with "claws and teeth grown perfect." The spilling of blood is a necessary condition of this idyllic state that "could not be the place / It is, without blood." If the animals' "soft eyes open," they are capable of ferocity, as well as of gentleness, "More deadly than they can believe." But the victims are spared both fear and pain since hunter and hunted alike flourish in a "sovereign floating of joy." "At the cycle's center," killing and being killed comprise a total love-relation, a fulfillment of animal life, since all beings are instantly reincarnated and reborn: "They fall, they are torn, / They rise, they walk again."

At times, Dickey's unqualified adulation for animals, like his glorification of the healthy-mindedness of children, verges on absurd romanticism. The vision in "The Heaven of Animals," however, as in most of Dickey's poems, works two ways. It suggests that man is the only corrupt animal. If he were removed from earth, beatitude would automatically transpire, just as it must have prevailed before his coming. The vision also anticipates later poems, beginning with "Fog Envelops the Animals," in which man the hunter tries to qualify for reentry into the animal heaven from which he has been excluded. To do so, he must purify himself, divest himself of all those aspects of humanness that unfit him for animal beatitude. The fog is the medium of purification: "Soundlessly whiteness is eating / My visible self alive. / I shall enter this world like the dead." As the visible self is eaten away, the fear and guilt of man the hunter are dissolved. Despite the fact that he kills, he can feel innocent.

In the earlier poems, the action is symbolic ritual; in "Springer Mountain," the action is realistic narrative interrupted by the advent of miracle— a plunge into the mystical beyond. If the earlier poems offered symbolic justification of the master-slave relation between hunter and hunted, "Springer Mountain" converts that relation into an erotic encounter between two equal, but qualitatively distinct, beings. The man spontaneously strips off his clothes and runs joyously in the woods with the deer. The hunter expresses his love for the animal-being in a more direct intimacy than ever before. He approaches the deer on a strictly human level, expressing the ardor and laughter of exuberant human affection. In contrast, in "Fog Envelops the Animals," he entered the animal's life-sphere by giving up his human qualities entirely to the transforming symbolic fog. The gains for entry into the foreign element were balanced, or canceled, by losses of realism and human identity. There is a kind of emotional dishonesty in glorifying the animal's otherness and integrity of being while debasing one's own human otherness, as though it can be taken off and put back on with one's clothes. Thus in "Springer Mountain" a deeper honesty is exhibited than in earlier poems. Though the hunter has become farcical in his excessive attempt to assume the identity of the deer-beloved, he has retained his human personality, and even though he ludicrously overshoots his human limitations in trying to identify with the deer, he salvages a sizable reward:

> For a few steps deep in the dance
> Of what I most am and should be
> And can be only once in this life.

The ultimate lesson Dickey brings back from his poems would seem to be wisdom of being. The poems teach him how to be, and we may suppose he learns as much from blundered tries for impossible being as from the successes.

As a poem, "Springer Mountain" is less successful than "The Heaven of Animals," because it is less compact and less technically achieved. As the poem searches for a new experience, a further reach of vision, the rhythms fall into a decadent sing-song and the experience is diffused, not intensified. Also, the laughter in the poem occurs at the extremity, rather than at the center, of its experience. It does not become a controlling point of view, as does the comic spirit in later poems like "Power and Light" and "Encounter in the Cage Country," but the poem winds up a chapter in Dickey's art. Once he has loved a deer with personal intimacy, he can never return to the master-slave relation again. He has hunted "Deer for the first and last time." He is a man who has learned, irrecoverably, that a deep give-and-take exchange is possible between man and animal, an exchange that maintains the identity in separateness of each being. He is now ready to bring to the final and fulfilled meetings of "The Sheep Child" and "Encounter in the Cage Country" a full quotient of human personality.

But first, it remains for the speaker of the poems to stretch beyond human limits in another extreme direction. In "Reincarnation 2," man literally becomes a bird, not merely evolving certain bird-like characteristics as in earlier poems. Kafka has captured the horror of man's turning into an animal in "Metamorphosis"; Dickey evokes the beatitude of man reborn as animal. Gradually, in Dickey's vision, man has qualified for complete entry into animal heaven. In "Reincarnation 2," entry, following elaborate ritual initiation, is irreversible. Man reborn as a bird can never change back into man again, as he can in myths and fairy stories of human/animal interchange. Early in the poem, the man senses that he has been transformed into a bird, and that he must learn to live with it. He still has human feelings and ideas, so they must either become annexed to the new bird-instincts, bird-senses, and bird-spirit, or give place to them. On one level, the man gradually divests himself of all aspects of humanness as he learns his new life, wears his new bird-identity. On another, the entire experience is perceived through the human awareness of the author. So man-spirit and bird-spirit are wedded in the bird's body, much as owl-spirit and blind child's spirit had become wedded in the father's dream song in "The Owl King."

Somehow, the conception of "Reincarnation 2" seems too settled in advance, and the experience seems contrived. In "The Sheep Child," terror and sexual mystery achieve the focus and compression of experience the other poem lacks. Too much of "Reincarnation 2" is diffused in the bloodless void of philosophical abstraction, but one really believes the sheep child's vision because its identity is so palpable, so uniquely realized in language of passionate intensity:

> *I am here, in my father's house.*
> *I who am half of your world, came deeply*
> *To my mother in the long grass*
> *Of the west pasture, where she stood like moonlight*
> *Listening for foxes. It was something like love*

From another world that seized her
From behind, and she gave, not lifting her head

Out of dew, without ever looking, her best
Self to that great need. Turned loose, she dipped her face
Farther into the chill of the earth, and in a sound
Of sobbing   of something stumbling
Away, began, as she must do,
To carry me.

"The Sheep Child" develops in two movements spoken by two separate personae, the narrator and the sheep child, a method that recalls the method of "The Owl King," in which each of three speakers views an experience from a different angle of vision. The sheep child is a vastly better poet than the narrator, exceeding him as the superhuman exceeds the human. The narrator's introductory remarks are delivered with the maundering stammer of a southern yokel spinning a ghostly yarn. In his soliloquy (above), the sheep child maintains that the farm boy regarded his sheep-mate as a thing without being, selfless, defenseless, caught unawares. To couple with the sheep would be a mere extension of the act of masturbation, like coupling "with soft-wooded trees / With mounds of earth." Shrewdly, the sheep complies with this falsification of her role to trap the boy into completing the act of bestiality. The boy mistakes the female sheep's absorbed passiveness for indifference, for *"she gave, not lifting her head / Out of dew, without ever looking, her best / Self to that great need."* The ewe experiences a perfect fulfillment of being; the farm boy, "stumbling away," is sobbing, haunted, driven wildly afraid by the profundity of her experience. His fear is mixed with guilt for having committed the forbidden act.

The ewe takes her place alongside "Crazy Jane" in the gallery of mindless sexual heroines in modern poetry in English. The farm boy's amazement and terror at her unexpected passion dramatize, in an original and unpredictable way, the mystery and depth of female sexuality. Yeats provided religious-erotic motifs that anticipate this poem in "Leda and the Swan" and "The Second Coming." But while Yeats molds the poem around myths taken from Bible, folklore, or literary tradition, Dickey draws on legends concocted by nonliterate, superstitious people to curb the wildness of the young. The poem combines the supernatural otherness of nightmare with Ripleyesque shock effects, but the vision is so powerfully conceived that it escapes sensationalism.

If "The Sheep Child" opens up new possibilities for deepening man's sexual identity, "Encounter in the Cage Country" explores opportunities for deepening his spiritual identity in a worldly setting (in this poem, the zoo). "Encounter" succeeds because the fabulous experience occurs unexpectedly, in a completely mundane context. The astonishing recognition and exchange between the narrator and the leopard unmistakably carries the ring of truth. Mystical events very likely do seem to invade the author's worldly life, leaping into his experience where he least expects to find them. They strike him, and those witnesses who happen to be present and looking on, with crushing reality:

> Among the crowd, he found me
> Out   and dropped his bloody snack
>
> And came to the perilous edge
> Of the cage, where the great bars tremble
> Like wire. All Sunday ambling stopped,
>
> The curved cells tightened around
> Us all   as we saw he was watching only
> Me.

"Encounter" is a celebration of individual uniqueness. As in "Snakebite," the protagonist pictures himself as the *one chosen,* chosen by some mysterious intelligent agent in the universe who

> was given a life-
> mission to say to me hungrily over
>
> And over and over   *your moves are exactly right*
> *For a few things in this world: we know you*
> *When you come, Green Eyes, Green Eyes.*

Most of the poems that employ the theme of human/animal relations try to maintain a balance between emotional extremes of joy and terror. In "The Heaven of Animals" and "Springer Mountain," the terror is felt to be too easily contained, or counterbalanced, by the joy. An irrepressible terror is unleashed in "The Sheep Child." Finally, a truer balance between deepened emotions is achieved in the vision of "Encounter in the Cage Country," in which the comic spirit becomes a center of focus:

> at one brilliant move
>
> I made as though drawing a gun from my hip-
> bone, the bite-sized children broke
> Up   changing their concept of laughter,

> But none of this changed his eyes, or changed
> My green glasses. Alert, attentive,
> He waited for what I could give him:
>
> My moves   my throat   my wildest love,
> The eyes behind my eyes.

While the humor enhances the seriousness of the exchange between man and beast, it also balances the terror as the poem rises to a peak of spiritual transcendence.

In the earlier poems, Dickey supposed he could give up his human self to the animal realm. The human/animal encounter in the last poem of the series, "Encounter in the Cage Country," has become a medium through which his human limitations can be transcended, but in going beyond his human condition, he no longer transforms into a new, wholly other being; instead, he intensifies and deepens the human self by adding animal powers to it. He becomes more truly human by realizing and releasing animistic powers recognized to have been inherent in him all along but not available until the fulfilled vision of the later poems. It is a vision which places the living man before us, a man whose daily experience may, at any moment, speak to him in the profound other-worldly language of dreams, a man who is instantly recognized by his spiritual kin among the animal kingdom, a man whose days are lit with wonders that never cease to amaze both himself and witnesses standing by, when they occur: "the crowd / Quailed from me   I was inside and out / Of myself."

RICHARD HOWARD

"We Never Can Really Tell Whether Nature Condemns Us or Loves Us"

Of the late Randall Jarrell, James Dickey once wrote, in his testy and cormorant collection of critical notes *The Suspect in Poetry:* "He gives you a foothold in a realm where literature itself is inessential, where your own world is more yours than you could ever have thought, or even felt, but is one you have always known." A close description of Dickey's own enterprise, and in its disputed tone (the essay on Jarrell is cast as a dialogue between the critic's warring allegiances to "form" and "life," each achievement "away" from literature being hotly and harshly opposed by the literary conscience, which is an impulse to get words down so they will not escape) a clue to this writer's ultimate yearning—that characteristic American tendency Emerson dramatized when he said "every new writer is only a new crater of an old volcano"—that yearning to transcend, by the flights and frauds of literature, literature itself, until the reader is separated from the writer by no more than his response to his own experience, and then united with that experience by a shared recognition of it.

The adventure of James Dickey's career, the pursuit of a poetry which must, in its transactions with love and death, self and circumstance, be as new as foam and as old as the rock (Emerson again), the heroic quest which is this poet's unending venture begins with an expression already complete, gorged on miracle and complacent as a sphere:

a way out of dying
Like a myth and a beast, conjoined.

From *Alone with America.* © 1980 by Richard Howard. Atheneum, 1980.

> More kinship and majesty
> Could not be,
> And nothing could look away.

in a first book of Orphic utterance, the meditative and metaphysical gno-
mons of *Into the Stone*, published on 1960. Here the poet has categorized,
divided up and dealt out, like so many divining suits, his first two dozen
poems into traditional categories: family, war, death and love. An imagery
of sociability, of killing and of ecstasy is thus the vehicle for ruminations on
life, death and resurrection, and so persuasive, so powerful is the plunge the
poet takes into the deep well of his discourse that wisdom survives the
interchangeability of the parts, vision sustains the replacement of elements,
and language, quite simply, serves:

> I sought how the spirit could fall
> Down this moss-feathered well:
> The motion by which my face
> Could descend through structureless grass,
> Dreaming of love, and pass
> Through solid earth, to rest
> On the unseen water's breast,
> Timelessly smiling, and free
> Of the world, of light, and of me.

Free of the world in this wise, the self would put off time and matter and
enter the universe of eternal being. But cannot, in safety, without the mediation of ritual, without the traditional politics of vision that hieratically
arranges matter (and matters), that ministers and officiates in such negoti-
ations with existence. The characteristic titles of Dickey's poems in this first
assay of "animal music"—titles that suggest the archetypal events and
symbols of the Grail legend: The Freeing of the Waters, The Fisher King,
The Hidden Castle, The Bleeding Lance—"The Underground Stream," "The
Vegetable King," "Into the Stone," "Walking on Water"—enforce the
boundaries of this poet's world of primaries in experience. Here is a construct of water in lakes and wells ("best motions come from the river"), gold
of metals and of the sun ("in this place where the sun is alone / the whole
field stammers with gold"), stone of the earth and of the alien moon ("the
night's one stone laid openly on the lost waves . . . a huge ruined stone in the
sky"). Here nothing develops, grows or changes from its essence, yet everything can be transformed into anything else, the metal sun and stone moon,
the winged tree and walking water woven into a net of correspondences

thrown over life like a tarnhelm. And the energy that knots these elements together, that thrusts them against each other in harmony or thematic opposition, is a circular movement, a conjugation of rituals: pieties of family, of kingship, of devotion to the divine Other, a round-dance of service and mastery best expressed, in terms of action, by the gerundive form. In the poetry of James Dickey, as he first composes it, there is no end to action, one is always in the process of it: "Awaiting the Swimmer," "Walking on Water," and most idiosyncratically, in the title of his second book, *Drowning With Others:*

> God add one string to my lyre
> That the snow-flake and leaf-bud shall mingle
> As the sun within moonlight is shining:
> That the hillside be opened in heartbreak
> And the woman walk down, and be risen
> From the place where she changes, each season,
> *Her death at the center of waiting.*

That is Dickey's Orpheus on his Eurydice, and the shape of it is typical: the concluding stanza of five, heavily yet loosely anapestic, finished off with a refrain, a repeated and ever-varying comment which refers the substance of the poem ("Orpheus Before Hades") to something very old and very early underlying it. Here the last line has been:

> *. . . Whose leaf is the center of waiting . . .*
> *. . . And white is the center of waiting . . .*
> *. . . Where love is the center of waiting . . .*
> *. . . When flesh is the center of waiting . . .*

and by the time we reach Eurydice's *"death at the center of waiting"* we have a kind of morphology of the refrain as Dickey uses it, so that as the poet himself does in another poem, we can put the refrain lines together at the end of the poem and have yet another poem, a kind of mythographic gloss on the experience presented, a marginalia which accounts for and perhaps justifies the separate poem in this ritual universe. The device is one taken over from Yeats; the rhetoric Valerian:

> Like a new light I enter my life
> And hover, not yet consumed,
> With the trees in holy alliance,
> About to be offered up.

and the tone, caught from Roethke and perhaps from such contemporary French poets as Char and Supervielle, is achieved by the preponderance of

end-stopped lines, a succession of aphorisms that remind us of the earliest
wisdom-literatures and stun the mind thirsting for some Becoming by their
insistent fixities:

> I take my deep heart from the air.
> The road like a woman is singing.
> It sings with what makes my heart beat
> In the air, and the moon turn around.
> The dead have their chance in my body.
> The stars are drawn into their myths.
> I bear nothing but moonlight upon me.
> I am known; I know my love.

The entities combine but do not alter or elide. The dimensions of the grad-
ual, of growth—of time, in fact—are absent or are only an element, never a
dimension at all. The self has its absences in eternity, then *recurs* in time,
bearing its burden, for others, of transgression and forgiveness:

> Mother son and wife
> Who live with me: I am in death
> And waking. Give me the looks that recall me.
> None knows why you have waited
> In the cold, thin house for winter
> To turn the inmost sunlight green
>
> And blue and red with life,
> But it must be so, since you have set
> These flowers upon the table, and milk for him
> Who, recurring in this body, bears you home
> Magnificent pardon, and dread impending crime.

Yet even the crimes are not those of history, of *happening*, in which all
of life's messy ontogeny is possible, but of myth and ritual, forgiven or
punished by incantation, fixed into immutable categories of ascension
and disgrace, dissolved ultimately into the natural round of violence and
recurrence:

> Like the dead about to be
> Born, I watch for signs: by kings
> Escaping, by shadows, by the gods of the body
> Made, when wounded skillfully,
> And out of their minds, descending
> To the dead.

In this first book of Dickey's, then, there is an airless mastery, a sense of liturgical consummation, of life's chances being eliminated as we follow the self's necessary scheme, that is quite stifling: as in those adjectival tropics of Conrad's, nothing moves, every leaf attends the fatal moment when its life or its death is appointed. Accident is expunged, being made illustrious with fate:

> Those waters see no more
> Than air, than sun, than stone,
> And stare it blind; in love, in love.

One of the rare accommodations of circumstance these poems afford is, as we might expect, in a version of warfare. Himself a veteran of Air Force service in both World War II and the Korean War, the violence of war's demands makes an appeal, in every sense, to Dickey's understanding of honor, rank and vassalage, of the egalitarianism that is to be found within royal bonds:

> Each eye is equal in the mighty head
> Of military gold.

In these experiences, though, there is an opportunity for the singular event to appear, occurrence construed as the subject of narration rather than of ritual, and in the poem aptly called "The Performance" the tone moves toward prose, toward an incident remembered rather than merely rehearsed as it is separated out from an Eternal Return:

> The last time I saw Donald Armstrong
> He was staggering oddly off into the sun,
> Going down, of the Philippine Islands.
> I let my shovel fall, and put that hand
> Above my eyes, and moved some way to one side.

But that scene, too, is actually a visionary recital: the narrator imagines his imprisoned, about-to-be executed comrade in arms

> Doing all his lean tricks to amaze them—
> The back somersault, the kip-up—
> And at last, the stand on his hands,
> Perfect, with his feet together,
> His head down, evenly breathing,
> As the sun poured up from the sea
>
> And the headsman broke down
> In a blaze of tears, in that light

> Of the thin, long human frame
> Upside down in its own strange joy.

Even in the disjunct life, the captive fate, ritual prevails and the language
veers back into the cadences of incandescence, life is irradiated by formality
and degree; the round-dance presides over action as over suffering. Only
then, once the "performance" was staged, could Armstrong have risen:

> In kingly, round-shouldered attendance,
> And then knelt down in himself
> Beside his hacked, glittering grave, having done
> All things in this life that he could.

But to the degree that it accommodates a secular event, this poem is an
exception in the liturgies of *Into the Stone*—the rest pursue their celebration
in a world of Dying Gods, of which we know that Orpheus was a prime
avatar: "My eyes," Dickey writes, speaking in that personation, "my eyes
turn green with the silence . . . where love is the center of waiting." One
wonders how a poet came by such an initiation—could the desecrated
simulacrum of Southern courtesy have been still charismatic enough to help
him on? What inherited convention of tribal response has furthered such
intuitions of nature and duty? The only answer to such questions will be to
discover how the poet gets *out* of the magic circle he has traced, how he
escapes the hermetic music which already threatens to keep his mind from
the movements of selfhood:

> This is the time foresaid, when I must enter
> The waking house, and return to a human love
>
> . . . .
> That time when I in the night
>
> Of water lay, with sparkling animals of light
> And distance made, with gods
> Which move through Heaven only as the spheres
> Are moved: by music, music.

Two years after *Into the Stone* appeared, Dickey published his second congregation of poems—three dozen of them this time, two very long, and the
entire group constituting a movement toward the "productions of time"
Blake said eternity was in love with—an impulse to break out of the archetypal spirals and into a linear history. There is still the aspiration, of course,
to be free of the personal, what Shelley called "that burr of self that sticks

to one so," to win free of contingency into an existence that would be an endless ring of ecstasy and regeneration; still that effort to discern

> how my light body
> Falls through the still years of my life
> On great other wings than its own.

For the bulk of *Drowning With Others,* then, James Dickey is still a poet of process rather than of particular presences, and of presences rather than persons, in his apprehension of nature as of selfhood. As its title suggests, the poem "Inside the River" is indentured to Heraclitus, the master of flux and pattern over fixity and identification; and if even more of this volume's notes are struck after Roethke than upon French models, the confidence in his eventual release and the mastery of his fluviose meters are all the closer to Dickey's consciousness of his burden ("the effect of the poem is really in the rapt continuation") for suggesting the pre-Socratic sage:

> Crouch in the secret
> Released underground
> With the earth of the fields
> All around you, gone
> Into purposeful grains
> That stream like dust
>
> In a holy hallway.
> Weight more changed
> Than that of one
> Now being born,
> Let go the root.
> Move with the world
> As the deep dead move.
> Opposed to nothing.
> Release.   Enter the sea
> Like a winding wind.
> No.   Rise.   Draw breath.
> Sing.   See no one.

Plumbing the water's depth, rising with flame, lying upon the earth, moving in air—the elements and the actions that must embrace them afford Dickey his *gestus,* but life itself urges a new drama, a modelling of experience which conflicts, at last, with the intuition of recurrence, an "accident" which counters ceremony and courtesy. In the book's longest poem, *Dover: Be-*

lieving in Kings, which is a kind of grand romantic fantasia on themes of inheritance and dispossession, there sounds the same grave, tender voice, the same chatoyancy of refrain and repetition, so that where the first stanza ends:

> In the sackcloth and breast-beating gray
> *The king wears newly, at evening.*
> *In a movement you cannot imagine*
> *Of air, the gulls fall, shaken*

—the thirteenth concludes:

> it is I
> *The king wears newly, in lasting.*
> *In a movement you cannot imagine*
> *Of spells, the gulls fall, listening*

—and the final apostrophe turns it again:

> Who . . . goes up the cliffs to be crowned?
> *In a movement you cannot imagine*
> *Of England, the king smiles, climbing: running.*

It will be noted that there is the same dependence on the gerundive form, without subject or object, to imply perpetuation of the impulse itself. Yet in all this ritual action, the hieratic themes so rehearsed in nature that the world of water and stone, creature and plant, is an emblem of what runs to its source inside a man, there is a real event: the poet and his family, the wife and two sons to whom the book is dedicated, have driven "down the ramp from the boat," have "watched for channel swimmers / dim with grease, come, here, / to the ale of the shallows." There is a real woman in the poem, not a corn queen or Morgan le Fay, but "my wife," and the accidental motions of an individual life are allowed to resist, to oppose, to overcome finally the onset of myth and of a history that is static, Plutarchian:

> I hove my father to my back
> And climbed from his barrow, there.
> Pride helped me pick a queen and get a son.
> The heroic drink of the womb
> Broke, then, into swanlike song.
> One came with scepter, one with cup,
> One goatlike back'd, and one with the head of a god.

Such a world of swords and gyves, parricide and piety in the archaic surround of the Dover cliffs, can be contemplated but it can also be left behind;

the poet and his family get into the car and drive away, into their lives. Indeed most of the other poems in this book are vivid with the tension between the longed-for ritual and the lived reality, or the stress between an inherited ceremony and an unmediated response. The poet, in this latter case, walks outside his house, looking back at his family sitting on a screened porch:

> All of them are sitting
> Inside a lamp of coarse wire
> And being in all directions
> Shed upon darkness,
> Their bodies softening to shadow.

But by the poem's end the ritual transfiguration, always at the ready in Dickey's sensibility, has operated upon them, and that same shadow becomes:

> the golden shadow
> Where people are lying,
> Emitted by their own house
> So humanly that they become
> More than human, and enter the place
> Of small, blindly singing things,
> Seeming to rejoice
> Perpetually.

"So human that they become more than human"—that is one accommodation of the doxologizing vision. Another is the link between ritual and sport, especially when that sport is hunting, exploited in this book with a little more credit on the side of the quotidian, a little less assurance that selfhood must or even may be extinguished. Still, as in "Fog Envelops the Animals"—one of Dickey's most characteristic pieces and certainly one of the most original contemporary poems, as anything very old seems very original—the magical transcendence can function in a moment:

> My arrows, keener than snowflakes,
> Are with me whenever I touch them.
> Above my head, the trees exchange their arms
> In the purest fear upon earth.
> Silence. Whiteness. Hunting.

Here the abrogation of identity delivers being over to the purely gerundive; not "I am silent in a white world in which I hunt," but "Silence. Whiteness.

Hunting." From this focus upon action at the expense of agent, it is but a step to the universe of pure recurrence that is "The Heaven of Animals":

> And those that are hunted
> Know this as their life,
> Their reward: to walk
>
> Under such trees in full knowledge
> Of what is in glory above them,
> And to feel no fear,
> But acceptance, compliance.
> Fulfilling themselves without pain
>
> At the cycle's center,
> They tremble, they walk
> Under the tree,
> They fall, they are torn,
> They rise, they walk again.

Animal recurrence identifies the world, too, of Dickey's other long poem in this book of commonplace prayer, "The Owl King," whose first section, "The Call," was printed as an independent poem or invocation in *Into the Stone;* the poet has enlarged its primal scene:

> in a ring in a meadow
> Round a child with a bird gravely dancing,
> I hear the king of the owls sing.

and has thickened the progress of the naked ritual to an entire myth, as Cornford and Harrison discovered that the classical myths were developed to explain the primitive mysteries, to rationalize and thereby recover actions whose meanings were without an explanation. The narrative element in Dickey's art is furthered, too, in its propensity to enlarge liturgy into something more nearly approaching illumination ("all dark shall come to light"); observation of nature in the added sections "The Owl King" and "The Blind Child's Story" transform the rites of passage into a *Märchen:*

> Each night, now, high on the oak,
> With his father calling like music,
> He sits with me here on the bough,
> His eyes inch by inch going forward
> Through stone dark, burning and picking
> The creatures out one by one,
> Each waiting alive in its own

> Peculiar light to be found:
> The mouse in its bundle of terror,
> The fox in the flame of its hair,
> And the snake in the form of all life.

The longing, though, to be free of what is contingent, of the liable and limiting self lies inside this story nonetheless, its irreducible core and concept:

> I understand
> The voice of my singing father.
> I shall be king of the wood.
> Our double throne shall grow
> Forever, until I see
> The self of every substance
> As it crouches, hidden and free.

Until I see the self of every substance. To counter the thrust of such desperate visions, some saving sense of the appearances in James Dickey has summoned up William James's beautiful aphorism, and acted upon it: "The deeper features of reality are found only in perceptual experience." For a preponderant impulse in this second book is entrusted to the limited, contingent, questioning experience of an individual identity laboring to transform its husk into its spirit. There is a quality of sundered occasions, now, about the titles—still gerundive, but much more specific, as in "Hunting Civil War Relics at Nimblewill Creek," or "To Landrum Guy, Beginning to Write at Sixty," or "A Dog Sleeping on My Feet." There are portraits of temporal sites, like "The Salt Marsh":

> All you can see are the tall
> Stalks of sawgrass, not sawing,
> But each of them holding its tip
> Exactly where your hair
> Begins to grow from your forehead.
> Wherever you come to is
> The same as before.

About such an accuracy, such an incursion upon what may be known, there is an intensity and an inclusiveness which *earns* rather than merely surrenders to the inescapable leap into spirit:

> And nothing prevents your bending
> With them, helping their wave

Upon wave upon wave upon wave
By not opposing,
By willing your supple inclusion
Among fields without promise of harvest,
In their marvelous spiritual walking
Everywhere, anywhere.

From the magical submersions of *Drowning With Others*, the defrocked
poet rises or at least advances into a world without explicit ceremony,
conscious of his task and, dispossessed of his ministry, ready to confront his
heritage: he must invent his own.

In 1964 Dickey published another collection of poems, *Helmets*, which
confirmed him as the telluric maker Wallace Stevens had called for in proph-
esying that the great poems of heaven and hell have been written and the
great poem of the earth remains to be written. Here, more loosely cast in the
emblems of battle and quest, are the same gerundive preoccupations with
process, though they are now content with the poem as its own reward,
rather than as a magical charm or source of control over nature. The poet
is no longer a necromancer, a magus, but a man speaking to himself, for
others, as in "Approaching Prayer":

Hoping only that
The irrelevancies one thinks of
When trying to pray
Are the prayer
And that I have got by my own
Means to the hovering place
Where I can say

.   .   .   .   .   .

Using images of earth

.   .   .   .

That my stillness was violent enough,

.   .   .   .

That reason was dead enough
For something important to be:

That, if not heard,
It may have been somehow said.

One of the principal *images of earth* Dickey has always used is that of
the helmet, which gives this new book its title: the word itself affords a clue
to his major preoccupations, for it derives from two old verbs for protecting

and concealing—protection, in Dickey's world, against the energies of earth, and concealment against those of the Unseen, crown and prison both. In his first book, Dickey had spoken of death as "the deadly king in a helmet glowing with spines"; had spoken of war as "the mighty head of military gold"; in *Drowning With Others,* the poem "Armor" discusses the use and despair of such things as helmets:

> When this is the thing you put on
> The world is pieced slowly together
> In the power of the crab and the insect
>
> . . . .
>
> There is no way of standing alone
> More, or no way of being
> More with the bound, shining dead,
>
> . . . .
>
>   In the bright locust-shell of my strength
> I have let the still sun
> Down into the stare of the eyepiece
> And raised its bird's beak to confront
> What man is within to live with me
> When I begin living forever.

But in this new book, such sacramental intuitions are discarded, and the helmet is no longer part of the archaic armor of the knight errant, but now one "I picked from the ground, not daring to take mine off"—simply a helmet filled with water, a tin hat from which, in the battle's lull, the soldier drinks—not Galahad sipping from the grail, but a tired G.I.:

> I drank and finished
> Like tasting of Heaven,
> Which is simply of,
> At seventeen years,
> Not dying wherever you are.

He realizes he has "inherited one of the dead" with the water accepted from the empty helmet, and imagines travelling to the home of its former tenant, in California where the poet once lived, and there he might

>   walk with him into the wood
> Until we were lost,
> Then take off the helmet

And tell him where I had stood,
What poured, what spilled, what swallowed.

And tell him I was the man.

That impulse—to disarm and confront one's naked humanity—is what governs this entire book, its celebrations of life on earth and its imagined figures: "where my breath takes shape on the air / like a white helmet come from the lungs." The book begins with a group of poems corresponding, in their chthonic pieties, to earlier pieces: "The Dusk of Horses" is a pendent to "The Heaven of Animals" and a part of Dickey's Georgia bestiary or foxhound fables:

No beast ever lived who understood
What happened among the sun's fields
Or cared why the color of grass
Fled over the hill while he stumbled,
Led by the halter to sleep
On his four taxed, worthy legs.

just as "At Darien Bridge" refers back to the dream landscapes and heroic prowesses of "Near Darien" in the first book, *Into the Stone*. But where in the first poem concerned with this place the site is enchanted ground and everything seen or sensed is miracle, everything is *given:*

As I ride blindly home from the sun,
Not wishing to know how she came there,
Commanded by glorious powers:
At night by the night's one stone
Laid openly on the lost waves,
By her eyes catching fire in the morning.

in the new poem, even in its more particular title, we are afforded the circumstances, the details—that there is a bridge here built by chain-gangs laboring ankle-deep in the water, that as a child the poet had come here to watch them at work, that now the poet returns to the place and with the wedding band on his ring finger "recalling the chains of their feet" (for Dickey, marriage is a binding sacrament in every sense of the term, another limiting condition of selfhood), stands and looks out:

over grasses
At the bridge they built, long abandoned,

Breaking down into water at last,

> And I long, like them, for freedom
>
> Or death, or to believe again
> That they worked on the ocean to give it
>
> The unchanging, hopeless look
> Out of which all miracles leap.

The book is full of justice rendered to the visible world by a divining conscience ("Under the ice the trout rode, / trembling, in the mastered heart / of the creek, with what he could do") and echoes with a kind of morality collected from the instances of natural order, as in the luxuriant, leisurely triptych "On the Coosawattee," whose first section, *By Canoe through the Fir Forest*, concludes:

> While the world fades, it is *becoming*.
> As the trees shut away all seeing,
> In my mouth I mix it with sunlight.
> Here, in the dark, it is *being*.

The Wordsworth who fled the shape of the mountain when he had stolen a boat would have understood such sorting out of ethical conclusions from natural form and process. The second section, *Below Ellijay*, describes the corruption of the stream by a poultry-processing plant, through whose carnage the canoe advances:

> Until we believed ourselves doomed
> And the planet corrupted forever
>
> . . . .
>
> And could have been on the Styx
> In the blaze of noon, till we felt
> The quickening pulse of the rapids
> And entered upon it like men
> Who sense that the world can be cleansed
>
> . . . .
>
> And plunged there like the unborn
> Who see earthly streams without taint
> Flow beneath them
>
> . . . .
>
> As they dress in the blinding clothes
> Of nakedness for their fall.

Here Dickey has succeeded, in his account of the characteristic spiritual journey or *ascensus,* in reconciling the starkest vocabulary of transcendence

with the lush nature of the backwoods country. It is a moment of aston-
ishing equilibrium in the poet's long quest, enriched in the final section, *The
Inundation,* with a remembered rescue from the rapids by another
Wordsworthian figure, "the strange woods boy" Lucas Gentry:

> Who may have been the accepting spirit of the place
> Come to call us to higher ground,
> Bent to raise
> Us from the sleep of the yet-to-be-drowned,
> There, with the black dream of the dead canoe
> Over our faces.

In thematic control, in sureness of their subject, these are poems so resolved
that one would be at a loss—and quite happy to be there—to define the
point where the poet's abiding struggle with himself might be located, were
it not for the aura of incantation, of litany that Dickey still employs, even
though he has steadily, painfully rid himself of the ritual imagination. Or
rather, even though he has rejected the ritual as something given, and has
instead cast it ahead of himself as something to be found, invented. By the
end of *Helmets,* the litaneutical measure is disputed, the steady beat of the
three- and four-foot lines, altered only by dactyl or spondee teleutons, and
generally matching line length with sense unit, is breaking up. Moreover the
long, regularly shaped stanzas give way to clusters of verse separated in
arbitrary ways by blanks—as if the poet were reluctant to let the cadences
coincide with the reader's breath, but must hurry him on when he would
pause, slow him down just when he would gather momentum. What in the
earlier books had sunk, with great virtuosity in diction, indeed with what
Gide called a "diverse monotonie," into the ear to do its murmurous work
is now offered in a less convinced form, or turned, as in "Cherrylog Road,"
to less reverent purposes. In this comic poem about meeting a forbidden
sweetheart in an automobile graveyard, the dying fall is jacked up by a
certain refusal to go along with the old ceremonies; even as the Balcony
Scene is exchanged for the back seat of a "34 Ford without wheels," the
poet is dissatisfied, for his newfound charge, with his old resonances, his
mastered meters:

> We left by separate doors
> Into the changed, other bodies
> Of cars, she down Cherrylog Road
> And I to my motorcycle
> Parked like the soul of the junkyard

> Restored, a bicycle fleshed
> With power, and tore off
> Up Highway 106, continually
> Drunk on the wind in my mouth,
> Wringing the handlebar for speed,
> Wild to be wreckage forever.

Or perhaps this is only the final virtuosity of such diction, and as Eliot said, its pathos, to be able to articulate only in the formalities of what one knows what one is trying to find out: "one has learnt to get the better of words for the thing one no longer has to say, or the way in which one is no longer disposed to say it." There is, either way, a shellac of complacency that is showing a crackle in itself, for all its luster, in many of these poems by

> A middle-aged, softening man
> Grinning and shaking his head
> In amazement to last him forever.

Though Dickey will always retain, for strategic use, the rhythms he had early developed to be those in which he most naturally addresses himself, entrusts his consciousness to the language, it is evident that a formal metamorphosis must occur, after *Helmets,* to accommodate the other change, the transformation of ritual into romance, which Dickey has effected in his poetry:

> as though I myself
> Were rising from stone

> Held by a thread in midair,
> Badly cut, local-looking, and totally uninspired,
> Not a masterwork

> Or even worth seeing at all
> But the spirit of this place just the same,
> Felt here as joy.

That metamorphosis has occurred in Dickey's next book, *Buckdancer's Choice,* of 1965, and occurred with such a rush of impulse that the reader of the earlier collections, having come to expect the somnambulist forms of Dickey's imagination of recurrence, will be jarred by the immediacy, the brutality of disjunct actions, performed once and, however celebrated, done away with. There are, of course, reminders—"Fox Blood" and "War Wound" are two—of the old incantatory pieties, the magical world where

each Thing possesses the properties of Another, a world of available correspondences:

> Touched with the moon's red silver,
>   Back-hearing around
> The stream of his body the tongue of hounds
> Feather him. In his own animal sun
>   Made of human moonlight
> He flies like a bolt running home.

But for the most part, Dickey's universe, and the measures which accommodate and express his phenomenology of exchange, has ceased to be one
of eternal return, of enchantment. Instead, once out of eternity, the poet
confronts and laments (exults over) the outrage of individual death, of a
linear movement within time—each event and each moment being unique,
therefore lost. If the self can die, then others exist, survivors of what
Newman, in another connection, called an aboriginal catastrophe. Obsession, madness, excess: the burden of *Buckdancer's Choice* is altogether new
in this poet, and crowned, or ballasted, by a pervasive terror of extinction.
That is the penalty of the historical imagination; its reward is the awareness
of others, always incipient in this poet but never before, by the very system
of his discourse, explicit. In two of the poems about graves in this book, it
is notable that the poet speaks of that terror, and of that awareness. In "The
Escape," Dickey envisions his own gravestone:

> It is an open book
> Of cardboard and paper, a simulated Bible,
> All white, like a giant bride's,
> The only real pages the ones
> The book opens to.

This is on a grave he has previously seen in a country cemetery in Alabama,
where a young deer was standing among the tombstones, puzzling out the
"not-quite-edible words of the book lying under / a panel of the surf":

> I remember that, and sleep
> Easier, seeing the animal head
> Nuzzling the fragment of Scripture,
> Browsing, before the first blotting rain
> On the fragile book
> Of the new dead, on words I take care,
> Even in sleep, not to read,
> Hoping for Genesis.

How different is that hope, and the tentative rhythm it assumes, from the old certainties of regeneration of *Into the Stone*! Paired with it, in the other determination of mortality "The Common Grave," is the realization that beyond the individual death

> All creatures tumbled together
> Get back in their wildest arms
> No single thing but each other.

and the final constatation is the last we might have expected from Dickey the poet of Being "revealed tremendously / in its fabulous, rigid, eternal / unlooked-for role," for it is an acknowledgment of greater possibilities than the One contains:

> An oak tree breaks
> Out and shoves for the moonlight,
> Bearing leaves which shall murmur for years,
> Dumbfoundedly, like mouths opened all at once
> At just the wrong time to be heard,
>   *Others, others.*

Hoping for Genesis, believing in others (and no longer in kings)—these are the gerundive moments of Dickey's fulfilled consciousness. They are sustained by a compassion, in the shorter poems, unmatched by the old will-to-power and unwarranted by the old metric. There is more air around these words, more space between the lines. Even between the *words* in some of the poems, the blanks stretch, suggesting not only a pause in the reader's drone but a separateness in the writer's experience. The lines are either broken off short or very long, but nowhere, in the larger efforts, are there the assent-inducing rhythms of spiralling chant, the beautiful generalities of transfiguration. Here we get novelistic detail, as in "The Fiend," a poem explicitly about a voyeur:

Her stressed nipples rising like things about to crawl off her   as he
    gets
A   hold   on   himself.   With   that   clasp   she   changes   senses
    something
Some breath through the fragile walls   some all-seeing eye

or deliberately parted fragments, the natural rhythms sundered:

      the tops of the sugar
Cane soaring   the sawgrass walking:

>   I come past
> The stale pools left
> Over from high tide   where the crab in the night sand
> Is basting himself with his claws   moving ripples outward
> Feasting on brightness
>   and above
> A gull also crabs slowly,
> Tacks, jibes   then turning the corner
> Of wind, receives himself like a brother
> As he glides upon his reflection.

Those last two lines remind us of the old incantations given over, and suggest what we may gain by keeping awake: an ability to confront the body's death as well as the spirit's life, without lulling the mind to sleep by hypnotic rhythms, occult correspondences.

Certainly a most remarkable poem in Dickey's later work is "The Firebombing," a very long poem in which, as I read it, the same movement outward upon a real world, magic discarded like Prospero's, books drowned and the natural man acknowledged—dolefully, awkwardly, but inevitably—is rehearsed in terms of the poet's own past and present circumstances. (A new irony is afforded by the epigraph from Gunther Eich: how perfect that it should be a contemporary German poet who remarks that "after the Catastrophe, each man will claim that he was innocent!") At the same time that he, he the poet James Dickey, no other man, in a waking dream carries out a napalm raid upon Japan, "sitting in a glass treasure-hole of blue light," he reviews his own suburban life twenty years later:

> in this half-paid-for pantry
> Among the red lids that screw off
> With an easy half-twist to the left
> And the long drawers crammed with dim spoons.

The poem is, surely, Dickey's most complete statement of the magical life in its appalling triumphs (military rank and power a part of the Old Order of kingship and vassalage) over against the slow conquests and defeats of an undistinguished reality. Here the pilot works an unimaginable and soundless destruction:

> In a red costly blast
> Flinging jelly over the walls

though he himself is "cool and enthralled in the cockpit,"

> Turned blue by the power of beauty,
> In a pale treasure-hole of soft light
> Deep in aesthetic contemplation
>
> . . . .
>
> It is this detachment
> The honored aesthetic evil,
> The greatest sense of power in one's life
> That must be shed.

And much of the poem's body, like the poet's, is dedicated to such shedding. The narrator, even as he executes the "anti-morale raid," lives his later life, worrying about being overweight, about his house "where the payments / for everything under the sun / pile peacefully up," and about his responsibility:

> All this and I am still hungry,
> Still twenty years overweight, still unable
> To get down there or see
> What really happened.

The failure or the refusal to imagine apocalypse, to accept the burden of the magical infliction of harm: that is the real subject of this poem. "Absolution? Sentence? No matter; / the thing itself is in that." Thus out of the conflict of the ritual imagination with the variety and complexity of life lived day by day, Dickey has made his most engrossing poem, one which challenges morality by magic, and chastens myth by life's daily texture.

The conflict operates on other levels too, as in "Slave Quarters," the other long poem that frames this book at its other end; here the same speaker visits a ruined plantation, "in the great place the great house is gone from," and romantically muses on the Master he would have been, his erotic disclosures paralleled by his supposed failure to acknowledge his illegitimate half-Negro scions. The burden is the same as in "The Firebombing": "How to take on the guilt"; and the shock of recognition which the present must sustain when confronted by the old dispensation, the magical immoralities of the past, is the same too. The poet stands in the ruined place by the tidal inlet where

> The real moon begins to come
> Apart on the water
> And two hundred years are turned back
> On with the headlights of a car,

and wonders what

It would be like   what it has been
What it is to look once a day
Into an only
Son's brown, waiting, wholly possessed
Amazing eyes, and not
Acknowledge, but own?

The old aristocratic duties are absorbed into the characteristic liberal doubts,
the world in which "my body has a color not yet freed." History is a
nightmare from which the self, struggling yet damned, may not escape. The
wit of this poem and the broader humor of "The Firebombing" reveal a
tension, an ironic balance Dickey has seldom shown, and it is as remarkable
that he can encompass, in the first poem, a line like "my house / where the
lawn mower rests on its laurels" or one like "another Bomb finds a
home / and clings to it like a child" as that in "Slave Quarters" he can make
the joke about the headlights already quoted, a joke effected by a line break.
"Mangham," one of the middle poems of this book that points in diction
back to the earlier style, wrests free of that ceremoniousness by its humor,
its punning rueful account of an old geometry teacher's stroke; Mangham
died explaining:

what I never
Could get to save my soul: those things that, once
Established, cannot be changed by angels,
Devils, lightning, ice or indifference:
Identities! Identities!

And even in one of the book's somberest pieces there is a gayety, a sense of
relief which accompanies the daylight recognition of wreckage and despair.
"Pursuit from Under" is a nightmare poem about a boy who imagines
himself an arctic explorer on his southern farm, visualizing a killer whale
striking up through the ice at shadows, even while the child's August week-
ends are passed barefoot on "the turf that will heave, / and the outraged
breath of the dead, so long held, will form / unbreathably around the living." Like the old explorers, the boy—the boy he was—"had been given an
image / of how the drowned dead pursue us." Here Dickey again asserts, as
in the distance between the magical blue cockpit of the firebombing and the
suburban etiolation of his everyday life, and as in the separation of the
modern ruins from the antebellum rituals, what he knows to be the distinction between recurrence and reality; the dissension between an incantatory
ageless order of transcendence with its themes of hierarchy, immutability

and terror, and on the other, nearer side a prosaic, mortal accommodation of immanence with its themes of becoming, of change, waste and deperition. James Dickey has searched deep in himself and wide in the world for a criticism of eternity by history, of immortality by trapped lives, of sovereignty by freedom. He is the man who most deserves to say of himself, as he has said:

> the heart of my brain has spoken
> To me, like an unknown brother,
> Gently, of ends and beginnings,
> Gently, of sources and outcomes,

so that what was once "impossible, brighter than sunlight" becomes

Something like three-dimensional dancing in the limbs   with age
Feeling more in two worlds than in one   in all worlds the growing
    encounters.

In 1967, Dickey gathered 15 of the two dozen poems from *Into the Stone*, 25 of the three dozen from *Drowning With Others*, 22 of the two dozen from *Helmets* and—the proportions are an indication, surely, of preference—all the poems from *Buckdancer's Choice* (which had won the National Book Award in 1965) into a single volume which also included 24 new poems, "growing encounters" indeed, some of them grown to a knowledge extended immensely beyond an encounter, the whole constituting 300 large, close-set pages of poetry, a decade's work, a lifetime's achievement, though the poet was at publication of *Poems: 1957–1967* only 44—a middle-age hugely concerned, however, to triumph over death, "that eternal process / most obsessively wrong with the world" and hungering for any means (reincarnation, apotheosis, witchcraft or that reversal of the signs which mystics and surrealists alike salute) to transcend the mortal body:

> to be dead
> In one life is to enter
> Another   to break out   to rise above

—somehow to live, convulsively, explosively, in a gigantic, legendary sense ("Lord, let me die   but not die / Out") which even the makeshift ardors of a shifting make ("Adultery") seem, momentarily, to afford:

> death is beaten by hazardous meetings that bridge
> A continent. One could never die here
> Never die   never die.

The body of the new work is sensationally framed by two mythological set-pieces, "Sermon" and "Falling"—the former, one of those ecstatic southern *Märschen* hard upon the Io section of Faulkner's *Hamlet*, though with a characteristically Dickey flick of the lash:

>   get up   up in your socks and take
> The pain you were born for: that rose through her body straight
> Up from the earth like a plant, like the process that raised overhead
> The limbs of the uninjured willow.

its subject a backwoods romance of abduction, murder and deësis (the Paraclete figured by a motorcycle, of course), its speaker a "Woman Preacher leaving the Baptist Church," and its style, as one might expect, an inflammatory qualification of the poet's late prose disclosures, perforated yet prolonged, which exist within the precincts of poetry chiefly by an intensity of realization, an assertion wilder than any mere music, any measure which might be brought to bear on the segmented, limber phrases, the members:

>   understand how a man casts finally
> Off everything that shields him from another   beholds his loins
> Shine with his children forever   burn with the very juice
> Of resurrection: such shining is how the spring creek comes
> Forth from its sunken rocks;

and the latter, the closing poem, the most extreme of all Dickey's gerundive studies, a gorgeous unpunctuated exultation of 250 lines in which an airline stewardess, half Danaë, half Leda, falls three miles from a plane into Kansas:

>   All those who find her impressed
> In the soft loam   gone down   driven well into the image of her
>   body
> The furrows for miles flowing in upon her where she lies very deep
> In her mortal outline   in the earth as it is in cloud   can tell
>   nothing
> But that she is there   inexplicable   unquestionable   and re-
>   member
> That something broke in them as well   and began to live and die
>   more
> When they walked for no reason into their fields to where the whole
>   earth
> Caught her.

There is, certainly, a loves-of-Jupiter aspect to all Dickey's late work, an erotic mastery of metamorphosis by which he reconstitutes, in a narrative utterly without ritual, the very mythology he has been at such pains to disintegrate in his figures, his meters. Meanwhile the more quietly handled poems between these two giant performances (*performances* must be the word: the platform manner is not to be dissociated, henceforth, from the galvanic achievements of this veteran barnstormer who comes before his audiences "in renewed light, utterly alone!") recapitulate every subject, every *subjection* of identity to the chthonic energy, to that possession by the gods which Dickey has owned up to throughout his work in order to own it; and if they are poems still "possessing / music order   repose," they possess, as well, that difference for which Dickey is now so often reproached by the very admirers of his old hieratic stance, his Heraclitean status; it is a mistake to reproach the poet for precisely what he has determined to do— his titanic choice is to recast the entire burden of utterance ("as though to be born   to awaken to what one is / were   to be carried"), transforming what has been recurrent and therefore changeless to what is, merely, real and released. Sublimity has become the substance of things hoped for, fable has become faith:

> The words of a love letter,
> Of a letter to a long-dead father,
>
> To an unborn son, to a woman
> Long another man's wife, to her children,
> To anyone out of reach, not born,
> Or dead, who lives again,
> Is born, is young, is the same;
> Anyone who can wait no longer
>
> Beneath the huge blackness of time
> Which lies concealing, concealing
> What must gleam forth in the end,
> Glimpsed, unchanging, and gone
> When memory stands without sleep
> And gets its strange spark from the world.

PAUL RAMSEY

James Dickey: Meter and Structure

... the hard and frequently bitter business of discrimination, which is
not the wildness but the practicality of hope.
                                                                —JAMES DICKEY

James Dickey has an extraordinary lyric gift and has written some excellent
short poems which must rank him high among American lyric poets. His
best poems open on nature and on spirit. His short poems, however, are
better than his long poems and his later long poems are not as good as his
earlier ones. In this essay I wish to explain why, by discussing his metrical
forms, then discussing the principles of structure in his short poems and
showing how those principles apply in his longer poems.

METER: RISING TRIMETER

The metrical history of James Dickey can be put briefly and sadly: a
great lyric rhythm found him; he varied it, loosened it, then left it, to try an
inferior form.

The form of the rhythm is end-stopped rising trimeter, well described
by John Hall Wheelock in his introduction to Dickey's poems in *Poets of
Today VII* (Charles Scribner's Sons, 1960). By "rising" I mean verse in
which iambics and anapests predominate.

Why the form has such power can only partly be said. It is a clearly felt
isolatable rhythm which has a base more insistently felt than that of iambic
pentameter, yet capable of more significant variation than some other strong
rhythms, for instance dipodic or trochaic rhythms. The force can be appar-

From *James Dickey: The Expansive Imagination,* edited by Richard J. Calhoun. ©
1973 by Richard J. Calhoun. Everett/Edwards, 1973.

ent in a single verse as in Yvor Winters's remarkable one-verse poem "Sleep": "O living pine, be still!" Yet the effect is cumulative also, and shifts of pulsation are felt within and across verses.

Theodore Roethke was a master of this form (as of some others), a poet from whom Dickey admits to having learned much; but Dickey gains new and strange resonances of his own. Here is a passage from Roethke's poem "Her Words" (*The Far Field*):

> "Write all my whispers down,"
> She cries to her true love.
> "I believe, I believe, in the moon!—
> What weather of heaven is this?"
> "The storm, the storm of a kiss."

It is a magnificent lyric tune. Roethke reinforces the basic pattern by making strong stresses strong and important and light stresses light and quick, but varies the speed and the comparative intensity of strong stresses ("Kiss" is nicely touched, "storm" storms twice.)

Dickey slows the tune, and darkens it.

> "Sleeping Out at Easter" (first stanza)
>
> All dark is now no more
> The forest is drawing a light.
> All Presences change into trees.
> One eye opens slowly without me.
> My sight is the same as the sun's,
> For this is the grave of the king,
> Where the earth turns, walking a choir.
>
> All dark is now no more.

Dickey's poem moves much slower than Roethke's, is richer in sound (quantity, timbre, reinforcements), with more stress on metrically unstressed syllables, and with more parallels of verse shape. The first verse, though straight iambs, is very slow and resonant. Verses 2 and 3 and verses 5 and 6 have the same scansion, iamb anapest anapest (i a a) as does the intervening verse 4 except for its feminine ending. Verses 5 and 6 are parallel in movement word for word.

> My sight is the same as the sun's,
> For this is the grave of the king

Verses 4 and 7 have secondary stress, in verse 7 combined with the mid-foot pause ("turns, wak-"). Such verse is incantatory, ominous, rich. Little is said, much gravely hinted, and the power of hinting is in the rhythm, language, imagery, the unitive tone.

Dickey in other poems finds perceptive ways to alter the rhythm, as in the following brilliant passage from "Dover: Believing in Kings" (section 1, last three verses).

> *The king wears newly, at evening.*
> *In a movement you cannot imagine*
> *Of air, the gulls fall, shaken.*

The feminine endings offer new possibilities of counterworking rhythms. The second verse quoted is much lighter and quieter than one expects, and the third achieves a tremulous reversal of movement within the frame: the enjambment from the second verse, the three successive nearly level stresses, the pause have prepared for the shift of motion to the natural trochee of "shaken."

To move much further away from the base is to travel in the mists of a boundary. "Chenille" is a lovely poem (until the narrator intrudes himself in place of the earlier characters and contrives absurdities) which, in its best sections, does vary further, nicely.

> There are two facing peacocks
> Or a ship flapping
> On its own white tufted sail
> At roadside, near a mill   (section 1)

> A middle-aged man's grandmother
> Sits in the summer green light
> Of leaves, gone toothless
> For eating grapes better,
> And pulls the animals through   (section 4, vv. 4–8)

> With a darning needle:
> Deer, rabbits and birds,
> Red whales and unicorns,
> Winged elephants, crowned ants   (section 5)

These nice imaginings are rhythmically alive and within hearing distance of rising trimeter. Several verses scan as rising trimeter, namely section 1, verses 3 and 4; 4: 5, 8; 5: 3. Other verses (1.1, 4.1, 4.7, and 5.2) have three distinct accents; two others (4.6 and 5.1) are rising dimeter; hence only 1.2

and 5.4 are really foreign to the basic form, and they are graceful reversals rather than stumbles. These passages represent about the far limit of the varied form; and other passages of the poem go medleyed or flat. One may of course call such passages free verse; but however called the poem is unmistakably influenced by rising trimeter.

To move beyond the form might of course mean to find other oceans and other trees; but Dickey does not, in what I shall call for convenience his middle phase, make many new rhythmical discoveries. The basic form hovers near enough to be felt, sometimes to interfere, but lacks its earlier throbs and dire or delicate changes.

"Cherrylog Road" is an interesting poem in several ways, but rhythmically lax. The trimeter pattern is heard enough so that the poem is not in free verse or prose, but the ground beat is less firm and the variations less significant than in the previous examples. By my count, thirty-six of the one hundred and eight verses do not scan in the pattern. The ones that do not fit are 1.4, 2.2, 4.1, 4.6, 5.3, 5.6, 6.4, 7.1, 7.2, 7.3, 7.5, 8.1, 8.2, 8.5, 9.6, 10.1, 10.2, 10.3, 10.4, 10.5, 11.2, 11.4, 12.1, 12.6, 13.6, 14.2, 14.5, 14.6, 15.4, 15.5, 16.3, 16.4, 17.4, 18.2, 18.3, and 18.5. Of those only eleven have three stresses (2.2, 4.6, 5.3, 5.6, 6.4, 7.2, 7.5, 8.5, 11.2, 14.2, 14.5, 16.3) so that the poem does not classify consistently as 3-stress verse. Counts will vary a little from reader to reader, but the main point is firm: the verse is between rising trimeter and somewhere else, too near the base to escape, too far away to fit. His earlier poetry is, in rhythm, far more powerful; and the poem lacks the intense precisions of the best short-line free verse of H. D. or William Carlos Williams or Robert Creeley.

The earlier rhythms would not simply serve this poem, since they fit the incantatory, and this poem mixes the incantatory and the conversational: in neither element are the meters quite at home. The poem has a clear narrative line, some good (if as usual too much and too careless) detail, and some nostalgias easy to share. But its rhythms do not support its strengths.

Yet the middle phase can work well. "The Scarred Girl" is a better poem in almost every respect than "Cherrylog Road." For once, Dickey keeps to the perspective of another person without intrusion; for once, he praises righteousness. The idea and the detail of the poem are excellent (the "wise" modifying "silver" seems to me the only false note in the poem), and the rhythms quietly hold. If the poem were nearer the base, the gentle dignity would be lost; if it were nearer prose or lax free-verse, its glassy intensity would fade.

"Buckdancer's Choice" is a graceful and attractive poem, though the

conclusion is not so grandly nostalgic as it tries to be, and the rhythm has
its infelicities. I shall scan the second and third stanzas.

In the invalid's bed; by mother	a a i fem.
Warbling all day to herself	t i a
The thousand variations of one song;	i i i i i
It is called Buckdancer's Choice.	a t i
For years, they have all been dying	i a i fem.
Out, the classic buck-and-wing men	t t t t or
	a i i fem.

The second stanza is delicate and properly gentle; the iambic pentameter
with three main stresses is a quiet variation from the pattern rather than an
intrusion. But in the third stanza "Buck-" and "Out" grate. The rising
rhythm is too strong for the medial trochee "Buckdanc-" not to limp, the
"Out" is worse. The unexpected radical enjambment gives the word a thrust
it cannot bear. Rhythm, syntax, and meaning collide; one cannot rescue all
three.

In the middle phase Dickey often varies the line lengths, two-stress and
four-stress verses being the more frequent variants. He also uses 5-stress and
6-stress verses as variants, "Sled Burial, Dream Ceremony" being an impressive example. Here rising trimeter mixes with longer verses, pentameter
predominating. The effect is a counterpatterning of trimeter and pentameter, an effect strengthened by the ambiguity of stresses. Actual stress admits
many degrees; in scansion a syllable is metrically stressed or not. Hence,
unless stress is quite strong or rules govern counting (as they do in
accentual-syllabics), one may legitimately count stresses in accentual poetry
more than one way. Thus in this poem the verse "The coffin top still is wide
open" would scan, in the context of Dickey's earlier verse, as three-stress
verse, i a a fem; it can also more calmly scan i i t i fem. Such patterning is
hard to sustain but works here, combining plangency and calm. The rhythms
fit the quiet, somber narrative (Dickey's narrative voice is typically asser-
tive and often blatant) and the great strangeness of tone and detail in the
poem.

Dickey's rising trimeter has for its founding mood the darkly incantatory; variation within and from that form can temper, subtilize, weaken, or
undo the form's power, as I have tried by these examples to show. When
good, it is often very good; I have delighted in many of his poems for years.

METER: SUBDIVIDED LONG-LINE FREE VERSE

Dickey has used extensively only one other form, the subdivided long-line free verse which predominates in his more recent work. Long-line free verse is a good form, as is proved by poems by such well-known poets as Walt Whitman, D. H. Lawrence, Robinson Jeffers, and Theodore Roethke, and by a number of other poems including Anne Stanford's "The Riders." It works largely by rhetorical and grammatical parallelism, by sweep, and by accumulation; and its defects ape its virtues: it is open to careless and unheard writing, to facile parallelism and accumulations.

Subdivided long-line free verse raises a logical, hence poetic problem. Long-line and short-line free verse are both valuable forms, but radically distinct. If long-lines are subdivided, then either one has long-line or short-line verse, misprinted; or else some pattern exists in which the unit and sub-unit are consistently meaningful.

That such a two-level pattern is possible is proven by paragraphing. Paragraphs are units, sentences sub-units. The lack of an adequate theory for paragraphing or (after much linguistic effort) for sentences, does not keep good writers from using paragraphs and sentences well. Thus, subdivided long-line free verse, though puzzling to theory, might work well.

Still, writers have made sentences and paragraphs for a long, practiced time. Subdivided long-line free verse is a newer and queerer thing, the burden of proof on its makers and auditors. Unless one can feel a distinct and continued sense of the two levels of division, one is apt to have jerky, overstressed, over-paused prose. Further, one strength of good long-line free verse is the sense of continuity of movement throughout the long line; to lose the sweep is to do away with a major resource of the form.

So much a priori, for what it's worth. My experience of Dickey's verse of this sort leads to the same unhappy conclusion. I may add that I came to such poetry (1) liking much long-line free verse, (2) writing a good deal of it myself, and (3) admiring Dickey's poetry. If I was biased, it was not against the form.

The purpose of the form, in Dickey's own words (in *Babel to Byzantium*) is to give "presentational immediacy," as though experience came in little bursts or chunks or breathless gasps. Experience seldom does. For instance, falling (one of Dickey's poems in this form is called "Falling") is consecutive, although the thoughts of a falling person may be disjointed. A trite metaphor has some validity: consciousness is more like a stream than it is like bursts of breath.

Presentational immediacy is demonstrably an insufficient ideal for poetry, since great poetry gives us experience understood and illumined, not merely mimed or rushed forth. The ideal nonetheless has some real value; the question is whether the form is adequate to that ideal.

Dickey's "The Shark's Parlor" tells a story in the form. The story is told as straight remembered narrative, but is presumably a nightmare or partially sur-natural imaginings; it is told with bloodthirsty gusto. The story has power if many flaws, but the metrical form adds little and detracts much. The long verses have no consistent principle I can infer or intuit. They lack rhetorical and grammatical repetition; they lack long swells and rises; they lack continuity throughout the long verse; they lack any clear sound patterning that finds my ear. The subdivisions are a kind of extremely crude punctuation. The actual variety and phrasing and "pointing" in poetry or even in speech and good prose, is immense, and any system of rhetorical punctuation or spacing which attempts to show one how to read a passage is grossly inadequate. If one reads "The Shark's Parlor" the way it is spaced, one gets the impression of a hysterical sort of force, but such a reading becomes monotonous very swiftly: it is a bad way to read. Yet, if the spacing does not show how to read, what is it for? I have, in short, found no valid way to read or hear these poems.

"The Fiend" probably uses the technique best: it is a bland, strange, at times sur-natural, off-and-on humorous portrayal of a voyeur. In it the spacings represent natural speech pauses or give valid emphasis. They do little beyond what non-spaced printing would do, but that little helps. Also they probably reinforce the floating dreamlike disconnection of the man's mind, a mood more appropriate here than in some other poems of the kind.

In "The Sheep Child," for me one of the best of Dickey's poems, some interior spacing combines with the rhythms of the middle phase; here the spacing is at least harmless. In "The Birthday Dream," which is essentially a good prose poem, the spacing merely crudens the reading.

In several ambitious poems with internal spacing, the form aims to show different sorts of confusion: in "Coming Back to America" the confusion of a severe hangover (taken very solemnly); in "Reincarnation" the confused states of passing in and out of nature and death; in "Falling" the disconnected thoughts of a stewardess falling to her death; in "May Day Sermon" the sexual-hysterical rantings of an insane woman preacher. The best poems in our heritage do not praise confusion, though they admit its existence. These poems praise confusion; the meters compound without intensifying or illumining the confusion. The meters also encourage Dickey's worse faults, including carelessness and prolixity. The great talent remains, but inner power lessens.

METER: SOME OTHER FORMS

These two forms, though they predominate, are not all. In particular, the poems in the June 1969 issue of *Poetry* show new departures (which have not been followed up in some more recently published poems). "Blood" is in a charged and driven free verse; "Pine: Taste, Touch and Sight" combines the three-beat line with falling rhythms to create a mood which fits the eating gloom of the passage; and "The Cancer Match," though elaborately placed on the passage, is essentially prose, a lively, dramatic, and highly rhythmical prose; it is a very good prose poem. Prose poetry, poetry in which rhythms work within verses, is a viable and little-used form worth some developing. The rhythms so achieved need not sound like ordinary prose rhythms at all.

Whether Dickey will go farther in any of these three good directions, is yet to see. His abundant talent, energy, and perception deserve better form than they have found in his kind of long-line free verse.

STRUCTURE: THE SHAPING OF LYRICS

In order to illustrate the principles of his shorter poems, I shall construct a blank verse "sonnet" with concluding rhyme, from one verse from each of fourteen of his poems, altering only punctuation.

> I bear nothing but moonlight upon me
> As I ride blindly home from the sun.
> Coming back, coming back, going over,
> I can stand only where I am standing,
> Unstable, tight-lipped, and amazed.
> I have been given my heart
> Holding onto myself by the hand
> In a gaze from a stone under water,
> Now a lake, now a clamoring chorus
> In a blaze of tears, in that light
> Of the ruined, calm world, in spring.
>
> My blind son stands-up beside me
> For this is the grave of the king.

(Respectively:

> "Into the Stone," st. 5, v. 7
> "Near Darien," st. 8, v. 1
> "On the Hill Below the Lighthouse," st. 7, v. 1

"Awaiting the Swimmer," st. 2, v. *5*
"Walking on Water," st. 7, v. *4*
"Trees and Cattle," st. 6, v. *5*
"The Other," st. 1, v. 1
"Poem," st. 11, v. 1 [in *Poets of Today* VII]
"Uncle," st. 1, v. 4 [in *Poets of Today* VII]
"The Performance," st. 7, v. 2
"The Vegetable King," st. 6, v. 4
"The Game," st. *5*, v. 1 [in *Poets of Today* VII]
"Sleeping Out at Easter," st. 1, v. 6)

The strange thing is that that "poem" is impressive poetry, and even has one kind of real coherence of development: the narrative of the soul moving in levels and illuminations. The "I" takes a journey in and out of mystery, into and out from a dream kingdom, the kingdoms of death, nature's strangeness, the levels of the soul. He makes discoveries of himself as he travels through different elements (air, water, sun, moon) and comes to feel nearer to other people and to God and nature, his own blind son rising very startlingly beside him as he arrives at the grave of the king.

That one can make a poem with that much coherence and consistency of style from different poems of his, shows how much repetition of theme and image and metrical effect there is in a range of his work. It also shows that such structure is not a fully narrative Aristotelian structure, nor an argumentative structure, nor a movement of inner necessity, organic form, since I clearly worked from the outside in making it. Granting the convention of themes, images, feeling, rhythm, the movement within the general idea of journey, of discovery is quite open. Any move within the tones and themes is possible. That kind of structure is not the only kind he uses in his short poems, but it is important and basic to them. One can illustrate this by looking at a poem of his, "Sleeping Out at Easter," in which the last stanza consists, movingly and credibly, of lines repeated from various places earlier in the poem. Only in his kind of structure could such a thing happen. Anyone who has ever tried to write a sestina or villanelle knows that about all one can do with the forms is to vary themes within some unity of mood. His forms are freer than those restrictive ones, but associative, thematic development is crucial within them. "Sleeping Out at Easter," one of the most beautiful and resonant of his poems, is as near the extreme of that method as any of his poems, though much less extreme than some brilliant poems of Roethke's.

Two other, overlapping methods of his short poems are (1) seminarrative of an experience, moving back and forth between and among certain objects or beings in the experience, a crisscross method, and (2) direct narrative of an experience, itself literal but conveying various suggested meanings beyond the literal in different ways than normal allegory. The first of these two is exemplified by "Trees and Cattle." A man looks at trees and cattle in sunlight and realizes something of his own nature and the nature of inner and outer reality. Some of the detail is natural ("A cow beneath it lies down"), some metaphorical ("I have been given my heart"), some speculative ("And fire may sweep these fields"), and some sur-natural ("my bull's horns die / From my head"). The shifts between the kinds of language are intricate with the structure. In general the poem happens in one specific place, giving a unity sustained and strengthened by tone, by romantic-religious meaning, and by crisscrossing between the objects and beings in the poem—sun, trees, cattle, I—in a way that feels highly patterned though unpredictable in advance.

Imagine a game played with several posts in a field, the rule being that one may move in any way back and forth between the posts but must touch each post at least twice and must not walk outside of them. Such a game would be less ruled, and consequently less fun, than baseball or—to leave the analogy—than a play by Shakespeare, but it would be much more formal than a game in which one wandered at random in a postless world among land and clouds vanishing into undersea creatures. Dickey's poem works like such posts and clouds, but the posts dominate and the sense of completed design is considerable. The confusion in the poem is contained. A good many of Dickey's shorter poems are like this, many of them using as posts present sensations juxtaposed with certain memories.

"The Driver" is much more straightforward. The narrator, an American soldier on a Pacific island just after World War II, goes joyously swimming. He sees a rusted half-track sunk ten feet under the water, swims down to it, sits in the seat, imagining what it was like to be the driver who he presumed died underwater when the half-track sank. He thinks of life, of death, of pure spirit, stays almost too long, then bursts, frightened, to the surface, seeing the sunlight which goes "for thousands of miles on the water." All works within the narrative frame; the narrative is graceful and persuasive; the analogies are natural rather than forced, the language and the rhythm beautiful. It is a beautiful poem, developed differently from the also excellent lyric "Sleeping Out at Easter." Both techniques are powerful and successful, as can be the crisscross method, which combines them.

These three methods are not the only methods Dickey uses in the short poem, but they are important and central. They all (even "The Driver," since the thoughts of the narrator could be of any length) are indefinitely expansible. They are methods for short poems.

Dickey's problem in the long poem is that those methods are virtually all he has to build with, and are not enough.

"The Owl King" is in my judgment his best longer poem, perhaps because it is the most darkly lyric of them, the most his sort of poem. It is about death and darkness, a world where strangeness is its own being and possession seeks love, but is blind. A blind son dies, goes to live with an owl king, is sought by the father whom he in turn seeks and evades. Three parts are spoken by the father, the owl king, and the son, and the journeyings of spirit are the longings of love. It is a wonderfully strange poem, and the movements to and fro between death, childhood, nature, life, are sufficiently all, so that no more normal shape of narrative is needed. No necessary limit is given to such a poem; it could be two lines or go on endlessly, but the sense achieved of arrived form and length seems powerfully right. This poem is near to the method of "Sleeping Out at Easter," but given more shape by the narrative of search and by the shifts of speakers. Three beings are in important relation, not just the one being who occupies most of Dickey's romantic, egoistic poetry. Even if the three beings are part of a subself, they still create a felt strength of relation often lacking in his work.

"Drinking from a Helmet" is in form like "The Driver" but much expanded. In each poem a soldier takes a helmet off the ground to drink at a water truck in a forward combat zone, leaving his own on for protection. As he drinks he imagines he comes (or does become) one with the spirit of the dead soldier. He finally puts on the other soldier's helmet, has a vision of the other soldier as a boy in California carrying his younger brother on a bicycle. As a consequence of the vision he imagines that he will, after the war, seek out the brother of the dead soldier.

The idea may be sentimental, but I find it appealing, and much of the poem is well done. But the poem is much longer in length, nineteen sections and 169 lines, than it is in substance; and most of it concerns the "I," the dead soldier getting comparatively few lines. Astonishingly the message that the "I" plans to convey to the younger brother is "tell him I was the man," the "I," not the dead brother. What could have been a very good poem is wrecked by expansion of the form, by intrusion of the ego over the meaning (which also accounts for the length—the ideal romantic egoist would find his sensations endlessly interesting), by being—in Roethke's good phrase— "too glib about eternal things," and by inaccurate and absurd detail. The last fault is frequent in Dickey's work; see the perceptively harsh discussion by Harry Morris in the Spring 1969 issue of the *Sewanee Review*. "The Driver," shorter by over a hundred verses, is the larger poem.

Many of Dickey's situations for poems are brilliant, and many others are skillful. "A Folk Singer of the Thirties" has a powerful and startling protagonist, a mythical figure well invented; a hobo guitarist nailed to the outside of a boxcar by railroad bulls to travel the length and breadth of America for a long time. Taken down by charitable orphans, he preaches to America out of his suffering experience, then at last sells out to TV and to the rich. Such a poem could be any length and stored with any American details. The conclusion (selling out) is only lightly realized, almost an afterthought. The travelling and much of the detail is strongly done and well proportioned. What disappoints is the preaching. The prophet seems to preach power as such: power of water, oil, whiskey; the rest is vaguely odd but mostly vague. The prophecy, the heart of the poem, is vacant. The poem reminds us how little actually Dickey has to *say*. The poetic theory implicit in his poems and pointed to here and there in his criticism is that poetry should only present experience intensely and immediately, not comment or offer understanding. The theory is false, but even if true, would not help in this instance: a preacher has to say something.

The failure to offer understanding wrecks the conclusion and invades the shaping of "The Firebombing," which is in many ways, despite numerous faults of detail, a powerful poem. The structure is achieved by the crisscross method: the poem juxtaposes memories of bombing Japanese civilians with napalm and the sensations of the pilot in an American suburb twenty years later, with only a little comment. The method of the poem, the switching back and forth, offers some good moments of tenderness, penance, and perceptive irony, but mostly offers a disquieting mixture of confusion and of *celebration* of the intensity of the events. The poem deals with a major issue, the bombing of civilians, but comes to no terms with it. The poem in fact denies the hope of coming to any such terms, ending thus:

> "Absolution? Sentence? No matter;
> The thing itself is in that."

But guilt and forgiveness, moral understanding and penance, social and individual, do matter, very greatly. The mere assertion of experience does not override them. If the last verse means that experience cannot be judged, or that the intensity of experience is what matters (which would make the bombing good not only for the pilot but for the children burnt to death— being burnt to death is an intense experience), then I profoundly disagree. And I imagine he means something like that, means "The thing itself is the thing itself." But one cannot tell what the last verse means; the reference of the pronoun is too incompetent to yield a meaning. The carelessness is not a mere smudge; it typifies the failure of the method. The poem, pretentiously, has nothing to say.

"Falling" and "May Day Sermon" are progressively worse examples of his methods. "Falling" recounts the imagined sensations and attitudes of a stewardess (apparently an actual person, the epigraph being a brief quotation from a newspaper account) falling to death from an airliner when an emergency door opened. It does not occur to the poet that the young woman's surviving friends or family (or she herself—Dickey believes in the survival of the spirit after death, his poems often tell us) may properly be offended at her death being used as a vehicle for such imaginings. What she felt and thought we do not know; it is neither likely nor pleasant to think that she played at being sky-diver, bat, hawk, stripteaser aiming at seducing all the farm boys and men in Kansas, on the way to her death.

James McConkey also deals in *Crossroads* (E. P. Dalton, 1968) with a person falling to death from an airplane. The comparison is instructive; and I would respectfully request the many people who admire Dickey's poem to read McConkey's humane and tender passage thoughtfully.

"May Day Sermon to the Women of Gilmer County, Georgia, by a Woman Preacher Leaving the Baptist Church" has the presumptive excuse that it is narrated by a ranting sexual maniac. Madmen of course can be powerful in literature; one only has to think what William Faulkner or Flannery O'Connor might have made of the narrator's or the protagonist's situation to realize how poorly the poem is developed and performed. The poem consists mostly of a crudely violent mixture of sexual, biblical, and Georgia country detail repeated in various similar hysterical-obscene-blasphemous patches crowded with ridiculous detail, including one-eyed twigs. Among the jumps and screams of the narrator's mouthings, a story is told, told very badly and with pointless obscurity. A farmer finds a used condom in a gully somewhere; he takes that to be sufficient evidence against his daughter, drags her out to a barn and/or a sapling (simultaneously or seriatim matters not), ties her and whips her ferociously while shouting Scripture at her. She screams hatred and defiance at him, boasting of her frenzied lovemaking. She later apparently kills her father with either an icepick or a pine needle in the eye, rides off on a motorcycle with her lover, taking off and throwing on bushes her clothes as they travel (a good acrobatic trick). The lovers ride off the earth, yearly, to a screaming, hysterical, passionate eternity of motorcycle riding, not even apparently ever stopping to make love. The poem applauds evil and (by name) hell. One may hope its absurdities undo its evangelism.

The poem is in plot line a wildly formless retelling of "The Eve of Saint Agnes." A careful comparison of the two poems, in beauty, intelligibility, structure, quality of imagination and development, moral insight, tenderness, and lovingness should reveal to any thoughtful reader something of the history of romanticism. In serious truth, since there is evil in the world, seeking the greatest intensity of experience is not a sufficient ideal. Dickey has said in *Metaphor as Pure Adventure* (Library of Congress, 1968) that the poet is "absolutely free" to "write according to laws of . . . /his own devising." Yes, but not free to write well.

More to the present point, a chief reason that this poem is a very bad poem, by a strongly talented poet who has written very good poems, is a failure in understanding the principles by which good or great long poems are possible.

JOYCE CAROL OATES

Out of Stone, Into Flesh

Despair and exultation
Lie down together and thrash
In the hot grass, no blade moving.
　　　　　—DICKEY, "Turning Away"

A man cannot pay as much attention to
himself as I do without living in Hell
all the time.
　　　　　—DICKEY, *Sorties*

The remarkable poetic achievement of James Dickey is characterized by a restless concern with the poet's "personality" in its relationships to the worlds of nature and of experience. His work is rarely confessional in the sense of the term as we have come to know it, yet it is always personal—at times contemplative, at times dramatic. Because Dickey has become so controversial in recent years, his incredible lyric and dramatic talent has not been adequately recognized, and his ceaseless, often monomaniacal questioning of identity, of the self, of that mysterious and elusive concept we call the personality, has not been investigated.

Yet this is only natural: it is always the fate of individuals who give voice to an era's hidden, atavistic desires, its "taboos," to be controversial and therefore misunderstood. Dickey's poetry is important not only because it is so skillful, but because it expresses, at times unintentionally, a great deal about the American imagination in its response to an increasingly complex and "unnatural" phase of civilization. (To Dickey mental processes have come to seem "unnatural" in contrast to physical acts: hence the "Hell" of

From *New Heaven, New Earth: The Visionary Experience in Literature.* © 1974 by Joyce Carol Oates. The Vanguard Press, 1974.

the quote from his journal, *Sorties*.) He has said, quite seriously, that "the world, the human mind, is dying of subtlety. What it needs is force" (*Sorties*, Garden City, New York, 1971). His imagination requires the heroic. But the world cannot and will not always accommodate the hero, no matter how passionately he believes he has identified himself with the fundamental, secret rhythms of nature itself. One comes to loathe the very self that voices its hopeless demands, the "I" that will not be satisfied and will never be silent. *I myself am hell* is a philosophical statement, though it is expressed in the poetic language of personal emotion.

The volumes of poetry Dickey has published so far—*Into the Stone* (1960), *Drowning With Others* (1962), *Helmets* (1964), *Buckdancer's Choice* (1965), *The Eye-Beaters, Blood, Victory, Madness, Buckhead and Mercy* (1970)—present a number of hypothetical or experimental personae, each a kind of reincarnation of an earlier consciousness through which the "self" of the poet endures. He moves, he grows, he suffers, he changes, yet he is still the same—the voice is a singular one, unmistakable. It asks why, knowing the soul heroic, the man himself is so trapped, so helpless? Dickey's central theme is the frustration that characterizes modern man, confronted with an increasingly depersonalized and intellectualized society— the frustration and its necessary corollary, murderous rage. Dickey is not popular with liberals. Yet one can learn from him, as from no other serious writer, what it is like to have been born into one world and to have survived into another. It might be argued that Dickey is our era's Whitman, but a Whitman subdued, no longer innocent, baptized by American violence into the role of a "killer/victim" who cannot locate within his society any standards by which his actions may be judged. A personality eager to identify itself with the collective, whether nature or other men, can survive only when the exterior world supports that mystical union of subject and object. Dickey speaks from the inside of our fallen, contaminated, guilt-obsessed era, and he speaks its language.

This was not always so: his earliest poems are lyric and meditative. They present a near-anonymous sensitivity, one hypnotized by forms, by Being in which dramatic and ostensibly intolerable truths are resolved by a formal, ritualistic—essentially magical—imagination into coherent and well-defined unities; his later poems submit this sensitivity to a broken, overheated, emotionally and intellectually turbulent world. The "stoneness" of the first volume undergoes an astonishing variety of metamorphoses until, in "The Eye-Beaters" and "Turning Away: Variations on Estrangement," it emerges as stark, isolated, combative self-consciousness, in which "A deadly, dramatic compression / Is made of the normal brow." The poet begins as Prospero, knowing all and forgiving all, and, through a series of sharply tested modes of perception, comes to seem like Hamlet of the great, tragic soliloquies.

Who can tell us more about ourselves?—about our "American," "masculine," most dangerous selves? Even more than Whitman, Dickey contains multitudes; he cannot be reproached for the fact that some of these aspects of a vast, complex self are at war with the others. He experiments with the art of poetry and with the external world and the relationships it offers him (will he be lover?—murderer?—observer?), but what is most moving about his work is his relentless honesty in regard to his own evolving perception of himself, the mystery of his "personality." He refuses to remain in any explored or conquered territory, either in his art or in his personality. Obsessed with the need to seek and to define, he speaks for those who know that the universe is rich with meaning but are not always able to relate the intellectual, conscious aspect of their natures to it. Thus, the need to reject the "conscious" mind and its public expression, civilization itself, which is so disturbing in Dickey. Indeed, *Sorties* is very nearly a confession of despair—the poet seems unable to integrate the various aspects of his nature, conceiving of the world of the intellect and art as "Hell." "Believe me, it is better to be stupid and ordinary," Dickey tells us early in the book. What such a temperament requires, however, is not less intelligence, but more.

Dickey has not always expressed himself in such extreme terms, and he has been, all along, a careful craftsman, knowing that meaning in poetry must be expressed through language, through a system of mental constructs. In fact, it must be invented anew with each poem; it must be rigorously contracted, abbreviated, made less explosive and less primitive. In an excellent essay in *The Suspect in Poetry* he cautions young poets against abandoning themselves to their unconscious "song," which he defines as "only a kind of monstrousness that has to be understood and ordered according to some principle to be meaningful." The unrestrained and unimagined self must be related syntactically to the external world in order to achieve meaning.

Yet the phenomenal world changes; language shifts, evolves, breaks free of its referents; and the human ego, mysteriously linked to both, is forced to undergo continuous alterations in order simply to survive. In the poem "Snakebite" (1967) the "stage of pine logs" and the "role / I have been cast in" give way suddenly and horribly to the dramatic transition from the pronoun "it" to the pronoun "me" as the poet realizes he is confined in his living, breathing, existential body: he is not playing a role after all. If he wants to survive he will have to drain that poison out of his bloodstream. Therefore, one of the burdens of the poet's higher awareness is to discover if there is any metamorphosis, any possible reincarnation, that is ultimately more than a mode of perception, *a way of arranging words.* Otherwise we begin to imagine ourselves as totally "estranged." To deny that estrangement we must deny our very framework of perception—language and sanity and logic—as if, by annihilating the mental construct of incarnation, we might somehow experience it on a level far below consciousness. Certainly Dickey has emphasized the poem as physical experience; he has set up opposing pseudocategories of the poetry of "participation" and the poetry of "reflection" (*Sorties*). Such an estrangement rests, however, upon the metaphysical assumption that man's intellect is an intruder in the universe and that the language systems he has devised are not utterly natural, natural to his species. Surely the human invention or creation of language is our species' highest achievement; some psycholinguists speculate that human beings are born with a genetic endowment for recognizing and formulating language, that they "possess genes for all kinds of information, with strands of special, peculiarly human DNA for the discernment of meaning in syntax." Failing to accept the intellect as triumphantly human, rather than somehow unnatural, the poet is doomed to endless struggles with the self. The "variations on estrangement" at the end of *The Eye-Beaters* deal with countless battles and meadows strewn "with inner lives," concluding with the hope that the poet's life may be seen "as a thing / That can be learned, / As those earnest young heroes learned theirs, / Later, much later on."

An objective assessment of one's situation must be experienced apart from life itself, then. And only "much later on." To use a critical term Dickey appropriated from Wordsworth, he is a poet of the "Second Birth," not one who, like Rimbaud or Dylan Thomas, possessed a natural instrument for poetry but one who eventually reduces the distinction between "born" and "made" poets only by hard work, by the "ultimate moral habit of trying each poem, each line, each word, against the shifting but finally constant standards of inner necessity" (*The Suspect in Poetry*). Contrary to his instinct for direct, undiluted self-expression, the poet has tried to define and develop his own personality as a "writing instrument"; he has pared back, reduced, restrained the chaotic "monstrousness" of raw emotion in order to relate his unique experience to common experience. He contradicts Eliot's ideal of an impersonal poetry, yet paradoxically refuses to endorse what he would call the monstrousness of confessional verse: "The belief in the value of one's personality has all but disappeared."

But what is personality, that a belief in it might save us?

Not a multileveled phenomenon, Dickey's sense of "personality," but rather a series of imagined dramas, sometimes no more than flashes of rapport, kinships with beasts or ancient ancestors—as in the apocalyptic "The Eye-Beaters," in which personality is gained only when "Reason" is rejected in favor of primitive action. The process of increasing self-consciousness, as image after image is explored, held up like a mask to the poet's face, absorbed, and finally discarded, comes to seem a tragic movement, as every existential role in the universe must ultimately be abandoned.

"INTACT AND INCREDIBLE LOVE"

Dickey has said that the century's greatest phrase is Albert Schweitzer's "reverence for life." This conviction runs through his work but is strongest in the earliest volumes. *Into the Stone* consists of contemplative, almost dreamlike poems that investigate the poet's many forms of love: beginning with the mythical, incantatory dissolution of the individual personality into both "dark" and "light" and concluding with the book's title poem, which emphasizes the poet's confident "knowing" and his being "known" through his relationship with a woman.

"Sleeping Out at Easter" is terse, restrained, as the "Word rising out of darkness" seems to act without the deliberate involvement of the poet. As dawn arrives in the forest, the "Presences" of night turn into trees and "One eye opens slowly without me." Everything moves in its own placid, nonpersonalized pattern, out of darkness and into the sunlight, and the world is "made good" by the springing together of wood and sun. The metamorphosis of Presences into daytime trees is one that could occur without the poet's song, yet the poet voices a total acceptance, as if he knew himself uniquely absorbed in the cycle of night/day, his "magical shepherd's cloak . . . not yet alive on [his] flesh." In other, similarly incantatory poems, the poet lies at the edge of a well, contemplating himself and his smile and the "grave face" of his dead brother, or lies "in ritual down" in a small unconsecrated grove of suburban pines—trying to get back, to get down, beneath both gods and animals, to "being part of the acclaimed rebirth" of spring ("The Vegetable King"). (Years later, when his poetry has undergone tremendous changes, Dickey will deal again with the transformation of a human being into a tree, in "The Fiend," one of his most eccentric poems.)

Into the Stone contains a number of war poems, but in spite of their subject they absorb the poet's personality much as the nature poems do, locating in confusion and panic certain centers of imagination, of decision, that the poet is able to recall years later, when "at peace." "The Enclosure" is the first of Dickey's many poems that "enclose" and idealize women: a group of war nurses on a Philippine island are protected by a compound with a wire fence, but the poet imagines them whispering to the soldiers outside "to deliver them out / Of the circle of impotence." In lines of curious, ceremonial calm the poet declares how, after the war, this vision led him to "fall / On the enemy's women / With intact and incredible love." Of the war poems, the most vivid is "The Performance," which celebrates the paradox of pain and triumph in the memory of David Armstrong, executed by the Japanese; Dickey remembers Armstrong doing a handstand against the sun, and his death by decapitation is seen as another kind of "performance." Even here there is a sense of acquiescence, finality, as if the cycle of nature could absorb this violent death as easily as it could absorb the shapes of trees back into primordial Presences.

The reverential awe of "Trees and Cattle" places the poet's consciousness in a "holy alliance" with trees, cattle, and sunlight, making his mind a "red beast"—his head gifted with ghostly bull's horns by the same magic that allowed Lawrence to imagine his head "hard-balanced, antlered" in "A Doe at Evening"; the sun itself burns more deeply because trees and cattle exist. A miracle of some kind has occurred, though it cannot be explained, and the poet half believes he may be saved from death; as, in a later poem, "Fog Envelops the Animals," the poet-hunter is somehow transformed into the "long-sought invisibility" of pure things or events or processes: "Silence. Whiteness. Hunting." But *Into the Stone* is characterized by passivity and no hint of the guilty, pleasurable agitation of physical life, whether hunting or love; the title poem describes the poet "on the way to a woman," preoccupied with a mystical absorption into the "stone" of the moon. The woman is outside the concern of the poem, undefined, not even mythologized; the poet is not vividly portrayed, as in "Cherrylog Road"; he could be any man, any lover, believing that "the dead have their chance in my body." All is still, mysterious, calm. The poet "knows" his place and his love, quite unlike the moon-drawn men of a later poem, "Apollo," who are seen as floating "on nothing / But procedure alone" and who symbolize "all humanity in the name / Of a new life." This later poem makes the "stone" of the moon into "stones," breaks up a seamless cosmology into a universe of "craters" and "mountains the animal / Eye has not seen since the earth split" (the earth-moon split an ancient and honored moon theory, of obvious symbolic, if not scientific, value)—not the Platonic oneness of stone, but stones:

We stare into the moon
dust, the earth-blazing ground. We laugh, with the beautiful
craze
Of Static. We bend, we pick up stones.

("Apollo")

A more dramatic sense of self is evident in Dickey's second book, *Drowning With Others*. Here he imagines the torturous memories of a lifeguard who failed to save a drowning child; he imagines himself inside the hunting dream of a dog sleeping on his feet; he contemplates fish in "The Movement of Fish" with the alert, awed scrutiny of Lawrence himself, making a judgment, like Lawrence's, that arises from the distant Otherness of the fish's world, where its sudden movement has the power to "convulse the whole ocean" and teach man the Kierkegaardian terror of the leap, the "fear and trembling" of great depths that are totally still, far beneath the superficial agitation that men see or float upon in their boats.

Yet the hunted/hunting animals of "The Heaven of Animals" are poetic constructions, Platonic essences of beasts wholly absorbed in a mythical cycle of life-death-rebirth: at the very center of nature these beasts "tremble," "fall," "are torn," "rise," and "walk again," like Emerson's red slayer and his perpetual victim. "The Heaven of Animals" is all but unique in Dickey's poetry because the poet himself has no clear position in it, as if its unity of Being somehow excluded an active intellectual consciousness; if we look back at the poem from "Fog Envelops the Animals" and other hunting poems and from Dickey's statements in *Self-Interviews* (Garden City, New York, 1970) about the mysterious "renewal" he experiences when hunting, we can assume that his deepest sympathies are with the predators, but this is not evident from the poem itself, which is one of his finest, most delicate achievements. The owl of "The Owl King" is another poetic (and not naturalistic) creature, a form of the poet himself who sits "in my shape / With my claws growing deep into wood / And my sight going slowly out, / Inch by inch." Superior forces belong to those who, like the owl, can see in the dark; or to those who, like Dickey himself, possess extraordinary powers of vision that set them apart from other, average men. But the forces are benevolent, godly, and restrained—the owl king participates in a mysterious ceremony with the blind child "as beasts at their own wedding, dance" and is not the symbol of cold, savage violence of the owl perched upon the tent in *Deliverance*, just as the poet-narrator of the volume *Drowning With Others* is not the helplessly eager murderer of *Deliverance*. Here, in the owl king's Roethkian kingdom, all nature is transformed by mind, its brutal contingencies and dreams suppressed, the possible "monstrousness" of its song made into a childlike lyric. Its final stanzas link it to earlier poems of Dickey's in which tension has been resolved by an act of impersonal, godly will:

> Far off, the owl king
> Sings like my father, growing
> In power. Father, I touch
> Your face. I have not seen
> My own, but it is yours.
> I come, I advance,
> I believe everything, I am here.

Through the child's (blind) acceptance, Dickey accepts the world; just as, in the anguished "The Eye-Beaters," he rejects the world of normal, rational vision, having been shaken by the experience of seeing blind children beat at their eyes in order to "see." In "The Owl King" the transcendent, paternal bird withdraws into the darkness of his own vision, while the lost child's father emerges, "In love with the sound of my voice," to claim his child; both aspects of the poetic consciousness are required if the child is to be saved, cherished, and yet both are dependent upon the child's acquiescence. (Just as, for the hunter, the imagined "acquiescence" of the hunted—the slain—is a ritualistic necessity; see Dickey's attempted justification of his love of hunting in *Self-Interviews*). This poem is a "song of innocence" whose unearthly simplicity—the child moves from tree to tree as if blessing them—will be transformed, years later, into the nightmarish "song of experience" of the crazed blind children in "The Eye-Beaters." Then, the objects of the poet's pity being, in themselves, hopeless, not even human children, beyond all love or language, the poet himself will narrowly escape madness. But this is years later, years deeper into flesh.

ENTERING HISTORY

In his third book, *Helmets,* Dickey begins to move out of the perfected world of eternal recurrence, no longer the awed, alert, but essentially passive observer, now ready to experience history. It is clear that Dickey desires to take on "his" own personal history as an analogue to or a microcosmic exploration of twentieth-century American history, which is one of the reasons he is so important a poet. In his inspired, witty, and ingeniously balanced essay on Randall Jarrell in *The Suspect in Poetry,* Dickey says he can discover in Jarrell's poetry very little excellence of technique, but he insists that Jarrell's contribution—"that of writing about real things, rather than playing games with words"—is a valuable one. Dickey indicates implicitly that *he* will take on both the challenge of being an artist and a historian of our era, which he has, applying a superior poetic talent to Jarrell's "realm ... of pity and terror ... a kind of non-understanding understanding, and above all of helplessness."

Once he is released from the sacred but bloodless cycle of nature, Dickey is concerned with giving life to this "non-understanding understanding" of creatures simpler than himself, or of an earlier form of himself, as in the beautiful, perfect poem, "Drinking from a Helmet." In "The Dusk of Horses" the emphasis has shifted from acceptance to a sharper awareness of distinctions between self and object, the need for the human participant in an action to judge it:

> No beast ever lived who understood.
>
> What happened among the sun's fields,
> Or cared why the color of grass
> Fled over the hill while he stumbled,
>
> Led by the halter to sleep
> On his four taxed, worthy legs.
> ("The Dusk of Horses")

In this and similar poems in *Helmets* the graceful fluidity of the lines is like the fluidity of the earlier poems: the god's-eye vision set to music. As the theme of "helplessness" grows, however, Dickey loses interest in well-made and sweetly sounding poetry and pours his remarkable energies into such extravaganzas of shouts and shrieks as "May Day Sermon." And where death might once have been resolved by a mystical affirmation of unity, in the recent poem "Diabetes" it is resolved by a surreptitious drink of beer; in "The Cancer Match," by whiskey.

Throughout *Helmets* there is an increasing growth, as if the subjects long loved by the poet are now shifting out of the hypnosis of love itself, beginning to elude his incantatory powers: coming alive and separate. In a poem reminiscent of Wallace Stevens's "Anecdote of the Jar," Dickey stands by a fence with his palm on the top wire and experiences a vision or a nervous hallucination of the disorder that would result if the tension of the wire were broken:

> If the wire were cut anywhere
> All his blood would fall to the ground

> And leave him standing and staring
> With a face as white as a Hereford's.
> ("Fence Wire")

The "top tense strand" is like a guitar string "tuned to an E," whose humming sound arranges the acres of the farm and holds them "highstrung and enthralled." Suddenly the poet in his human role must accept a position in nature which is superior to that of trees and cattle, an intellectual responsibility that will involve both exultation and the risk of despair. But because of Dickey's hand on this fence wire,

> The dead corn is more
> Balanced in death than it was,
> The animals more aware
>
> Within the huge human embrace
> Held up and borne out of sight
> Upon short, unbreakable poles
> Where through the ruled land intones
> Like a psalm.

Because of the sensational aspects of some of his later poems, Dickey is not usually known to have concerned himself so seriously, and so perceptively, with the metaphysics behind aesthetic action; it is characteristic of his energy and his pursuit of new challenges that a very few poems about "poetry" are enough for him. If read in its proper chronological place in Dickey's work, "Fence Wire" is a moving as well as a significant poem; it is the first clear statement of the poet's sense of himself as involved responsibly in history. In his most powerful poems the tension between that "top thread tuned to an E" and the abandonment to one's own possible, probable "monstrousness" provides a dramatic excitement generally lacking in these early, though entirely admirable poems, and less content with lyric verse itself, Dickey will experiment with wildly imaginative monologues in which words float and leap all over the page.

In *Helmets* there is also a new sense of exploration into an "Otherness," not a declaring of unities, analogues, "correspondences" between all phenomena in nature: Dickey stands "At Darien Bridge" and muses upon the chain-gang workers who built the bridge many years ago, when he was a child; he hopes to see a bird, the one bird "no one has looked for," and the scratched wedding band on his finger recalls the convicts' chains—like them, he longs for freedom, or even death, or at least the ability to believe again in "the unchanging, hopeless look / Out of which all miracles leap."

(In contrast to the miraculous vision of "Trees and Cattle.") In "Chenille" he encounters another kind of poet, an old woman who darns quilts endlessly, not ordinary bedspreads of the kind made by machine and sold in the normal world but quilts decorated with red whales, unicorns, winged elephants, crowned ants—"Beasts that cannot be thought of / By the wholly sane." Increasingly, the surreal intrudes into what should be the real, or sane; in "On the Coosawattee" Dickey and his companion on a canoeing trip are shocked to see how the water has been defiled by a poultry-processing plant upstream:

> All morning we floated on feathers
> Among the drawn heads which appeared
> Everywhere, from under the logs
>
> Of feathers, from upstream behind us,
> Lounging back to us from ahead,
> Until we believed ourselves doomed
> And the planet corrupted forever.

Though the two men shoot the rapids and finally escape this horror, the canoeists of *Deliverance* return to experience the river's mysterious dangers and the unhuman ground-bass of sound that becomes "deeper and more massively frantic and authoritative" as they continue—and this time not all will survive, and none will get back to civilization with anything like this poem's triumphant declaration of the human ability to escape other human defilement. In the blaze of noon the canoeists on the Coosawattee River feel

> The quickening pulse of the rapids
> And entered upon it like men
> Who sense that the world can be cleansed
>
> Among rocks pallid only with water,
> And plunged there like the unborn
> Who see earthly streams without taint
> Flow beneath them.

"Cherrylog Road" is the first of the unmistakably Dickeyesque poems: nostalgic and comic simultaneously, demystifying the love so laborously mystified elsewhere, even naming names ("Doris Holbrook") and giving directions:

> Off Highway 106
> At Cherrylog Road I entered
> The '34 Ford without wheels,

> Smothered in kudzu,
> With a seat pulled out to run
> Corn whiskey down from the hills.

And in this automobile graveyard the boy moves from car to car, delighted to be naming, placing, experiencing, without the need to make anything sacred or even essentially important: from the Ford to an Essex to a blue Chevrolet to a Pierce-Arrow, "as in a wild stock-car race / In the parking lot of the dead." He hopes his girl friend will come to him from her father's farm "And . . . get back there / With no trace of me on her face"; when she does arrive and they embrace, their love-making takes place in the same "stalled, dreaming traffic" as the hunting of mice by blacksnakes, and beetles soon reclaim the field of the car's seat springs. The narrator leaves on his motorcycle, which is unglamorized, "Like the soul of the junkyard / Restored, a bicycle fleshed / With power"—an earlier, more convincing version of the spectacular "May Day Sermon."

"The Poisoned Man" deals with the same situation explored in a later poem, "Snakebite" (from "Falling," in *Poems 1957–1967*) in which the victim of a poisonous snake is forced to cut himself with a knife in order to drain out the poison. In the earlier poem a formal, almost allegorical meaning evolves from the terrifying experience; the poet has a kind of vision, feeling that his heart's blood could flow "Unendingly out of the mountain." "Snakebite" reduces this visionary abstraction to "I have a problem with / My right foot and my life." Aging, the poet is urgently concerned with survival itself; he has called himself a poet of "survival." In another poem about snakes, "Goodbye to Serpents," Dickey and his son observe snakes in a Parisian zoo, and Dickey tries to concentrate on them as he never has in the past. His meditation is so complete that he seems to pass into them, seeing the human world of towers and churches and streets "All old, all cold with my gaze," and he longs to believe that he has somehow retained, at the same time, his own human presence, the human miracles of "self" and "love." But it is a failure:

> And I know I have not been moved
> Enough by the things I have moved through,
> And I have seen what I have seen
>
> Unchanged, hypnotized, and perceptive.

Unchanged, hypnotized, and perceptive: a strange combination of words. But in the first of Dickey's "reincarnation" poems in a later volume, *Buckdancer's Choice,* he becomes a snake with head "poisonous and poised." Perhaps he is suggesting that the very awe of nature that mesmerized him has prevented his being "moved" humanly by the things he has experienced. The mystic's world of total acceptance has always contrasted sharply with the world of human suffering.

Helmets concludes with one of Dickey's most remarkable poems, the little-discussed "Drinking from a Helmet." The young narrator, in wartime, drinks from a helmet he picked up near his foxhole and sways "as if kissed in the brain," standing

> as though I possessed
> A cool, trembling man
> Exactly my size, swallowed whole.

He throws down his own helmet and puts on the one he has found, an inheritance from the dead. Then he seems to "see" in his own brain the dying man's last thought—a memory of two boys, the soldier and his older brother in a setting of tremendous trees "That would grow on the sun if they could." Where "Approaching Prayer" traced what seemed to be the poet's conscious effort to imagine a dying hog's experience, "Drinking from a Helmet" seems sheer unwilled vision:

> I saw a fence
> And two boys facing each other,
> Quietly talking,
> Looking in at the gigantic redwoods,
> The rings in the trunks turning slowly
> To raise up stupendous green.
> . . . .
> I would survive and go there,
> Stepping off the train in a helmet
> That held a man's last thought,
> Which showed him his older brother
> Showing him trees.
> I would ride through all
> California upon two wheels
> Until I came to the white
> Dirt road where they had been,
> Hoping to meet his blond brother,
> And to walk with him into the wood
> Until we were lost,
> Then take off the helmet

> And tell him where I had stood,
> What poured, what spilled, what swallowed:

> And tell him I was the man.

The relationship between the two brothers is interesting, because it reverses the relationship of Dickey and his own older brother, who evidently died before Dickey was born. (See "The Underground Stream," "The String," and other poems, in which the "tall cadaver" of the brother is summoned up by the poet, who believes himself conceived by his parents "out of grief" and brought to life "To replace the incredible child" who had died. The psychologically disastrous results of such a belief, if sincere, hardly need to be examined; one is always a "survivor," always "guilty," and always conscious of being an inferior substitute for some superior being.) Here, the younger brother has died and Dickey himself will go to visit the surviving older brother, as if, somehow, both he and his older brother were living and able to speak to each other; a life-affirming magic, in spite of a young soldier's death.

MONSTERS

After *Helmets* Dickey's poetry changes considerably. The colloquial tone and unserious rhythms of "Cherrylog Road" are used for deadly serious purposes as Dickey explores hypothetical selves and the possibility of values outside the human sphere. Where in an early poem like "The Performance" a mystical placidity rendered even a brutal execution into something observed, now most actions, most states of being, are examined bluntly, brutally, emotionally, as the poet subjects himself to raw life without the sustaining rituals of Being.

Dickey has many extraordinary poems, fusions of "genius" and "art," but the central poem of his work seems to be "The Firebombing," from *Buckdancer's Choice*. No reader, adjusted to the high, measured art of Dickey's first three volumes, can be ready for this particular poem; it is unforgettable, and seems to me an important achievement in our contemporary literature, a masterpiece that could only have been written by an American, and only by Dickey.

"The Firebombing" is an eight-page poem of irregular lines, abrupt transitions and leaps, stanzas of varying length, connected by suburban-surreal images, a terrifying visionary experience endured in a "well-stocked pantry." Its effort is to realize, to *feel,* what the poet did twenty years before as a participant in an "anti-morale raid" over Japan during the closing months of World War II. Its larger effort is to feel guilt and finally to feel anything. One of the epigraphs to the poem is from the Book of Job: "Or hast thou an arm like God?" This is Dickey's ironic self-directed question, for it is he, Dickey, the homeowner/killer, the Job/God, who has tried on the strength of vast powers and has not been able to survive them. Irony is something altogether new in Dickey:

> Homeowners unite.

> All families lie together, though some are burned alive.
> The others try to feel
> For them. Some can, it is often said.

The detachment is not godly, but despairing. Though he is now Job, he was at one time the "arm of God," and being both man and God is an impossibility. Dickey's earlier war poems always show him a survivor, grateful to survive, rather boyish and stunned by the mystery of a strange rightness beneath disorder; it seems to have taken him many years to get to this particular poem, though its meaning in his life must have been central. Now the survivor is also a killer. What of this, what of killing?—What is a release from the sin of killing? Confession, but, most of all, guilt; if the poet cannot make himself feel guilt even for the deaths of children, how will it be possible for him to feel anything human at all?—

> some technical-minded stranger with my hands
> Is sitting in a glass treasure-hole of blue light,
> Having potential fire under the undeodorized arms
> Of his wings, on thin bomb-shackles,
> The "tear-drop-shaped" 300-gallon drop-tanks
> Filled with napalm and gasoline.

This stranger is, or was, Dickey himself, who flew one hundred combat missions through the South Pacific, the Philippines, and Okinawa and participated in B-29 raids over Japan; but he is only a memory now, an eerily aesthetic memory. He exists in the mind of a suburban husband and father, worrying about his weight and the half-paid-for pantry that is part of his homeowning and his present "treasure-hole":

> Where the lawn mower rests on its laurels
> Where the diet exists
> For my own good   where I try to drop
> Twenty years.

So many years after the event, what remains? He is now a civilian, a citizen, an American who understands himself in ironic, secret charge of all the necessary trivia of unaesthetic life—the purchasing of golf carts and tennis shoes, new automobiles, Christmas decorations—that he knows as the "glue inspired / By love of country," the means by which the possibly atomistic or death-bound ego is held fast in its identity. Though the wonder remains, he is far from the moon-hypnotized, somnambulistic rhythms of the past; "The Firebombing" is what Dickey would call an "open poem," one in which a certain compulsiveness in the presentation of the subject matter precludes or makes peripheral an aesthetic response, and the poet's own recollection of his action is mocked, if it must be assessed in stylized terms:

> As I sail artistically over
> The resort town followed by farms,
> Singing and twisting
> All the handles in heaven   kicking
> The small cattle off their feet
> In a red costly blast
> Flinging jelly over the walls
> As in a chemical war-
> fare field demonstration.

Remembering this, he knows that "my hat should crawl on my head" and "the fat on my body should pale"—but one of the horrors of this bombing raid is that it has somehow destroyed a normal human response, as if the "arm of God" the pilot had assumed had also annihilated him. Having shown us so convincingly in his poetry how natural, how inevitable, is man's love for all things, Dickey now shows us what happens when man is forced to destroy, forced to step down into history and be an American ("and proud of it"). In so doing he enters a tragic dimension in which few poets indeed have operated. Could Whitman's affirmation hold out if he were forced to affirm not just the violence of others, but his own? If war is necessary, warriors are necessary; someone must sacrifice his cosmic love; and not only is the traditional life-praising song of the poet savagely mocked by his performance as a patriot in wartime, but the poet cannot even experience his own deeds, for he has acted as a machine inside a machine. In "The Firebombing" everything must remain remote and abstract, not experienced in any vital way. The Machine Age splits man irreparably from his instinctive need to see, to feel, to *know* through the senses. The Whitmanesque affirmation of man is difficult to sustain if the poet can see the objects of his love only from a great height, through an intellectual telescope. When Whitman feels he is "on the verge of a usual mistake" ("Song of Myself," st. 38), it is only an emotional mistake; he could never have considered the nihilism of a self without emotions, in which his inventiveness could really attach itself to nothing because it could experience nothing.

After this dreamlike unleashing of "all American fire," the poet states flatly that *death will not be what it should*—a counterstatement, perhaps, to Schweitzer's *reverence for life*. This is the poet's unique vision:

> Ah, under one's dark arms
> Something strange-scented falls—when those on earth
> Die, there is not even sound;
> One is cool and enthralled in the cockpit,
> Turned blue by the power of beauty,
> In a pale treasure-hole of soft light
> Deep in aesthetic contemplation,
> Seeing the ponds catch fire
> And cast it through ring after ring
> Of land.
>
> . . . .
>
> It is this detachment,
> The honored aesthetic evil,
> The greatest sense of power in one's life,
> That must be shed in bars, or by whatever
> Means, by starvation
> Visions in well-stocked pantries.

These "visions" will inspire in the poet wilder and wilder imaginings in his own creative life and an abandonment of the ego as "homeowner" in favor of the ego as "hunter" or "primitive." The mechanized State tempts one to an aesthetic evil, and so perhaps salvation may be found in a pre-aesthetic, prehistorical animality that will seize upon possible rites (the structural basis of *Deliverance*) in order to exorcise the despairing and suicidal violence of the animal self. Whether Dickey's themes are explorative rather than absolute, whether his work traces an autobiographical query or a record, the function of his poetry seems to be the demonstration of the failure of such a vision. And yet it is certainly tempting to take on the viciousness—and the innocence—of the animal, to take for our totems owls, snakes, foxes, wolverines, and to reject forever the possibilities of detachment and evil that are inherent in civilization.

Like Dostoyevski, Dickey considers the helplessness of the *killer*. But, unlike Dostoyevski, he cannot imagine a transformation of the killer into a higher form of himself: the mysterious process by which Raskolnikov grows and by which Smerdyakov can be seen as a rudimentary form of Father Zossima. But Dickey cannot operate through metaphor, as Dostoyevski did, for he was the man, he did these things, *he* and no one else. Though his poetry charts a process of wonders, a changing of selves, finally he is only himself, a particular man, trapped in a finite and aging body with memories that belong to him and not to the rest of us, not to any liberalized concept of the guilt we all "share." (Like Marcuse, Dickey could probably feel no more than scorn for the "repressive tolerance" of some aspects of liberalism.) If made general and universal, in order to be shared, is guilt itself not made an aesthetic event?—a luxury?—a perversion?

But the narrator of the poem cannot concern himself with such abstractions:

> All this, and I am still hungry,
> Still twenty years overweight, still unable
> To get down there or see
> What really happened.
>
> . . . .
>
> It is that I can imagine
> At the threshold nothing
> With its ears crackling off
> Like powdery leaves,
> Nothing with children of ashes, nothing not
> Amiable, gentle, well-meaning.

A poetry of Being can move to perfect resolutions, but this poetry of anguished Becoming cannot. ("Some can, it is often said," Dickey has remarked, ironically and sadly.) The narrative and confessional elements of "The Firebombing" demand a totally different aesthetic: the aesthetic-denying open form. No reconciliation of opposites is possible here because the poet cannot reconcile himself to his earlier self. And so what of "Absolution? Sentence?" These do not matter for "The thing itself is in that."

"The Firebombing" is central to an understanding of Dickey's work. It could not have been prophesied on the basis of the earlier, Roethke-inspired poems; but once it appears, unsuppressed, it is so powerful an illumination that it helps to explain a great deal that might remain mysterious and puzzling. *Buckdancer's Choice*, "Falling," and, above all, *The Eye-Beaters* deal with mortality, decay, disease, perhaps attributable in part to the poet's actual aging, but only in part, for the descent into a physically combative and increasingly unaesthetic world is not the usual pattern our finest poets follow, as both Roethke and Yeats, and other poets of the "Second Birth," suggest. Yet the emphasis Dickey places upon mortality, his self-consciousness about it, is a motif that begins to appear even in his literary criticism. How is it possible that the man who believes in nature—in natural processes—should feel uneasy about the natural process of aging? It is a paradox in Hemingway also, but perhaps it is to be understood in Rilke's terms: our fear is not of death, but of life unlived. In an introduction to Paul Carroll's *The Young American Poets* (Chicago, 1968), Dickey makes a statement that totally contradicts the contemplative, balanced criticism of *The Suspect in Poetry* of only four years previous:

> The aging process almost always brings to the poet the secret conviction that he has settled for far too little. . . . The nearer he gets to his end the more he yearns for the cave: for a wild, shaggy, all-out, all-involving way of speaking where language and he (or, now, someone: some new poet) engage each other at primitive levels, on ground where the issues are not those of literary fashion but are quite literally those of life and death. All his lifelong struggle with "craft" seems a tragic and ludicrous waste of time.

One would imagine, from such remarks, that the speaker is far older than forty-five; "the nearer he gets to his end . . ." is a visionary statement that might be comprehensible in the Yeats of *Last Poems,* but astonishing in a poet who is the same age as the Yeats of *The Green Helmet.* But if a denial of "craft" (or civilization) is needed in order to release spontaneous energy, then one can see why, for Dickey, it must be attempted.

ENTROPY

Buckdancer's Choice received the National Book Award in 1965, and in 1967 Dickey put together his *Poems 1957–1967* for Wesleyan University Press. The *Poems* do not observe strict chronological order, however, beginning with the demonic "May Day Sermon to the Women of Gilmer County, Georgia, by a Woman Preacher Leaving the Baptist Church," one of Dickey's most flamboyant poems. Clearly, Dickey does not want the reader to enter the world of *Into the Stone* with the innocence he himself had entered it; that celebration of forms is all but outshouted by the eleven-page sermon, which is about violence done to and by a young girl in Georgia, and about her escape with her motorcycle-riding lover, "stoned out of their minds on the white / Lightning of fog"—

>   singing   the saddlebags full of her clothes
> Flying   snagging   shoes hurling away   stockings grabbed-off
> Unwinding and furling on twigs: all we know   all we could
>   follow
> Them by was her underwear   was stocking after stocking
>   where it tore
> Away, and a long slip stretched on a thorn   all these few gave
> Out. Children, you know it: that place was where they took
> Off into the air   died   disappeared   entered my mouth
>   your mind

It is an incredible achievement, with the intonations of a mad, inspired sermon, the flesh elevated beyond the spirit, but both elevated into myth. It is a myth that transforms everything into it: everything turns into everything else, through passion. The intellect exercises very little control in this "wild, shaggy, all-out, all-involving" work, and though Dickey has expressed doubt over the value of Allen Ginsberg's poetry, one is forced to think of certain works of Ginsberg's and of how, under ether sniffing or morphine injection, Ginsberg wrote all of *Ankor Wat* and that extravaganza "Aether," in which a preaching voice proclaims certain truths to us: "we are the sweepings of the moon / we're what's *left over* from perfection"—"(my) Madness is intelligible reactions to / Unintelligible phenomena"—
        And—

> What *can* be possible
> In a minor universe
> In which you can see
> God by sniffing the
> gas in a cotton?
>   ("Aether," in
>   *Reality Sandwiches*)

Dickey is much more violent, more heartless than Ginsberg, of course, since he is driven by energies more archaic than is Ginsberg, who is a philosopher with a respect for the syntax of the imagination if not of superficial grammar; the "May Day Sermon" is at once revenge for and repetition of the helplessness of the bomber pilot, a mythic annihilation of a punishing, near-invisible father, and an escape off into space, the girl's clothing cast off behind her like the airline stewardess' clothing in "Falling." In all the exuberant spurts of language there is violence, but especially here:

And she comes down   putting her back into
The hatchet   often   often   he is brought down   laid out
Lashing   smoking   sucking wind: Children, each year at this time
A girl will tend to take an ice pick in both hands   a lone pine
Needle   will hover   hover: Children, each year at this time
Things happen quickly   and it is easy for a needle to pass
Through the eye of a man bound for Heaven   she leaves it naked goes
Without further sin through the house.

After countless readings, "May Day Sermon" still has the power to shock: consider the "needle-eye-Heaven" joke. The maniacal repetitions make one wince ("get up . . . up in your socks and rise"), and the Dylan Thomas-surreal touches sometimes seem forced ("Dancing with God in a mule's eye"), but the poem's shrieking transmutation of murder, nakedness, eroticism, fertility, and poetry into a single event has an irresistible strength: "everything is more *more* MORE." Nature itself becomes active in the process of transmutation as even "peanuts and beans exchange / Shells in joy," and in a poetic sleight of hand reminiscent of Thomas's *Ballad of the Long-Legged Bait* at its apocalyptic conclusion, "the barn falls in / Like Jericho." The countryside itself is speaking through the woman preacher "as beasts speak to themselves / Of holiness learned in the barn." It is mysticism, but existential and ribald, noisy, filled with the humming of gnats and strange prophecies:

> Each May you will crouch like a sawhorse to make
>   yourself
> More here   you will be cow chips   chickens croaking
> . . . .
>   and every last one of you will groan
> Like nails barely holding   and your hair be full of the gray
> Glints of stump chains.   Children, each year at this time you
>   will have
> Back-pain, but also heaven.

In "May Day Sermon" Dickey creates a patchwork of images that go beyond the "not wholly sane" images of "Chenille."

However, *Buckdancer's Choice* contains several very personal and moving poems dealing with mortality, the title poem and "Angina" (which deal with Dickey's mother, an invalid "dying of breathless angina"), "Them, Crying," "The Escape," and one that reasserts the mystical possibility of transcending death, its certainties expressed in a steady three-beat line:

> All ages of mankind unite
> Where it is dark enough.
>
> . . . .
>
> All creatures tumbled together
> Get back in their wildest arms
> No single thing but each other.
>   ("The Common Grave")

But the most passionate poems are counterstatements concerned with developing images adequate to express horror; in "Pursuit from Under" the poet summons up a terrifying image that does not have its place in his own experience, or even in his probable experience, but is a conscious re-creation of a memory. He is standing in a meadow, in August, and imagines he hears the "bark of seals" and feels "the cold of a personal ice age." Then he recalls having once read an account of Arctic explorers who died of starvation and whose journal contained a single entry of unforgettable horror:

> under the ice,
>
> The killer whale darts and distorts,
> Cut down by the flawing glass
>
> To a weasel's shadow,
> And when, through his ceiling, he sees
> Anything darker than snow
> He falls away
> To gather more and more force
>
> . . . .
>
>   then charges
> Straight up, looms up at the ice and smashes
> Into it with his forehead.

And so the killer whale pursues the poet, even in this familiar meadow in the South, and he thinks of "how the downed dead pursue us"—"not only in the snow / But in the family field." It is interesting to note that Norman Mailer's nihilistic and very deliberately "literary" novel *Why Are We in Vietnam?* also transports its protagonist/victim to the Arctic in order to allow him a vision of God-as-beast; this "vision" is then imposed upon all of American (universal?) experience and can allow for no possibilities of transcendence. If God is a beast (as Dickey concludes in "The Eye-Beaters"), then the beast is God, and one must either acquiesce to Him and experience the helplessness of terror in an ordinary southern meadow, or imitate Him,

taking on some of His powers. But, increasingly, the poet reaches out beyond his own geographical and historical territory to appropriate this vision. It demands a distortion or a rejection of naturalistic life; at times, as
he admits, a kind of necessary theatricality, as he explains in *Self-Interviews*
why hunting is so important to him: "the main thing is to re-enter the cycle
of the man who hunts for his food. Now this may be play-acting at being a
primitive man, but it's better than not having any rapport with the animal
at all . . . I have a great sense of renewal when I am able to go into the woods
and hunt with a bow and arrow, to enter into the animal's world in this
way." And, in *Deliverance,* the experience of "renewal" or deliverance itself
is stimulated by a hunt for other men; simple animals are no longer enough,
and the whole of the novel is constructed around those several intensely
dramatic moments in which the narrator sights his target—a human and
usually forbidden target—and kills him with an arrow from his powerful
bow. The arrow is at least real; the napalm and gasoline bomb are not, since
they are dropped upon abstractions. And, too, the necessary intimacy of the
besieged men in *Deliverance* approximates a primitive brotherliness, ex-
cluding the confusion that women bring to a world of simple, clear, direct
actions. For women, while mysterious and unfathomable, are also "civilization."

But if women are objects, goddess objects, they too can be assimilated
into the mystique of primitive power-worship. One of the most striking
poems in all of Dickey's work is "The Fiend," which magically transforms
a voyeur/lover into a tree, into an omnipotent observer, back into a voyeur
again, while throughout he is the poet who loves and desires and despairs of
truly knowing his subject; the poem is a long, hushed, reverential overture
to murder. Yet the equation of the voyeur with the poet is obvious, and the
poem concludes ominously by remarking how "the light / Of a hundred
favored windows" has "gone wrong somewhere in his glasses." Dickey is
remarkably honest in acknowledging the value he puts upon his own fantasies, in contrast to the less interesting world of reality. What is important
is *his* imaginative creation, *his* powers of seeing. In praise of what a Jungian
would call the "anima," Dickey has said in *Sorties* that "poor mortal perishable women are as dust before these powerful and sensual creatures of
the depths of one's being." A dangerous overestimation of the individual's
self-sufficiency, one might think, especially since there is always the possibility of that interior light going "wrong somewhere in his glasses."

In fact, in Dickey's later poems eyesight becomes crucial, aligned with
the mysterious grace of masculinity itself. When one's vision begins to
weaken, there is an immediate danger of loss of control; conversely, "sight"

itself can be rejected, denied, as a prelude to glorious savagery. Or the denial
of vision can facilitate a more formal, sinister betrayal, as Dickey imagines
himself as, simultaneously, a slave owner on a southern plantation and the
white father of an illegitimate black son and the father-who-denies-his-son,
a master driven to madness by his role as an owner, in the poem, "Slave
Quarters." Dickey's question concerns itself with many forms of paternal
betrayal, a betrayal of the eyes of others:

> What it is to look once a day
> Into an only
> Son's brown, waiting, wholly possessed
> Amazing eye, and not
> Acknowledge, but own.

How take on the guilt . . . ? is the poem's central question.

In the section "Falling" in *Poems 1957–1967*, Dickey explores further
extensions of life, beginning with "Reincarnation 2," in which the poet has
taken on the form of a bird. His first reincarnation was into a snake, which
we leave waiting in an old wheel not for food but for the first man to walk
by—minute by minute the head of the snake becoming "more poisonous
and poised." But as a bird the poet undergoes a long, eerie, metaphysical
flight that takes him out of mortality altogether—

> to be dead
> In one life is to enter
> Another   to break out   to rise above   the clouds

But "Reincarnation 2" is extremely abstract and does not seem to have
engaged the poet's imaginative energies as deeply as "Reincarnation 1" of
Buckdancer's Choice. It is balanced by the long "Falling," an astonishing
poetic feat that dramatizes the accidental fall of an airline stewardess from
a plane to her death in a corn field. "The greatest thing that ever came to
Kansas" undergoes a number of swift metamorphoses—owl, hawk, goddess—stripping herself naked as she falls. She imagines the possibility of
falling into water, turning her fall into a dive so that she can "come out
healthily dripping / And be handed a Coca-Cola," but ultimately she is
helpless to save herself; she is a human being, not a bird like the spiritual
power of "Reincarnation 2," and she comes to know how "the body will
assume without effort any position / Except the one that will sustain
it   enable it to rise live / Not die." She dies, "driven well into the image of
her body," inexplicable and unquestionable, and her clothes begin to come

down all over Kansas; a kind of mortal goddess, given as much immortality by this strange poem as poetry is capable of giving its subjects.

The starkly confessional poem "Adultery" tells of the poet's need for life-affirming moments, though they are furtive and evidently depend upon a belief that the guilt caused by an act of adultery is magical—"We have done it again   we are / Still living." The poem's subject is really not adultery or any exploration of the connections between people; it is about the desperate need to prove that life is still possible. *We are still living:* that guilty, triumphant cry. In this poem and several others, Dickey seems to share Norman Mailer's sentiment that sex would be meaningless if divorced from "guilt." What role does the woman play in this male scenario? She is evidently real enough, since she is driven to tears by the impossibility of the adulterous situation; but in a more important sense she does not really exist, for she is one of those "poor mortal perishable women" temporarily illuminated by the man's anima-projection, and she is "as dust" compared to the fantasy that arises from the depths of the lover's being. Descartes's *I doubt, hence I think; I think, hence I am* has become, for those who despair of the Cartesian logic of salvation, *I love, hence I exist; I am loved, hence I must exist.*

With Dickey this fear is closely related to the fundamental helplessness he feels as a man trapped in a puzzling technological civilization he cannot totally comprehend. Even the passionate love of women and the guilt of adultery will not be sufficient, ultimately, to convince the poet that he will continue to exist. He identifies with the wolverine, that "small, filthy, unwinged" creature whose species is in danger of extinction, in the poem "For the Last Wolverine." The wolverine is an animal capable of "mindless rage," enslaved by the "glutton's internal fire," but Dickey recognizes a kinship with it in the creature's hopeless desire to "eat / The world."

Yet, for all its bloodthirsty frenzy, the wolverine is in danger of dying out. It is a "nonsurvivor" after all. The poet's mystical identification with this beast is, paradoxically, an identification with death, and death driven, indeed, is the impulse behind his musing: "How much the timid poem needs / The mindless explosion of your rage." Like Sylvia Plath and innumerable others, the poet imagines a division between himself as a human being and the rest of the world—the universe itself—symbolized by the fact that his consciousness allows him to see and to judge his position, while the rest of nature is more or less mute. It is doubtful, incidentally, that nature is really so mute, so unintelligent, as alienated personalities seem to think; it is certainly doubtful that the human ego, the "I," is in any significant way isolated from the vast, living totality of which it is a part. However, granted for the moment that the poet is "timid" when he compares himself to the most vicious of animals, it is still questionable whether such viciousness, such "mindless explosion" of rage, is superior to the poem, to the human activity of creating and organizing language in a coherent, original structure. The prayer of the poem is very moving, but it is not the wolverine's consciousness that is speaking to us: "Lord, let me die   but not die / Out."

Dickey has dramatized from the inside the terrors of the personality that fears it may not be immortal after all; its control of itself and of other people and of the environment seems to be more and more illusory, fading, failing. "Entropy"—a much-used and misused term—refers to the phenomenon of energy loss and increasing disorder as a system begins to falter, and is always a threat, a terror, to those who assume that the system to which they belong or which they have themselves organized was meant to be infinite. There is no space here to consider the psychological reasons for the shift from man's assumption of immortality as an abstraction (the "immortal" soul was expected to survive, but not the "mortal" man—the personality or ego) to his frantic and futile hope for immortality in the flesh. There are cultural, political, economic reasons, certainly, but they cannot entirely account for the naïveté of the wish: *I want to live forever*. Because this wish is so extraordinarily naïve, even childish, it is never allowed in that form into the consciousness of most intelligent people. When it emerges, it is always disguised. It sometimes takes the form of a vague, disappointed despair; or rage without any appropriate object; or a hopeless and even sentimental envy of those human beings (or animals) who strike the despairing one as too stupid to know how unhappy they should be. The excessive admiration of animals and birds and other manifestations of "unconscious" nature is, in some people, a screen for their own self-loathing. They are in "hell" because the activity of their consciousness is mainly self-concerned, self-questioning, self-doubting. The rest of the world, however, seems quite content. As entropy is irrationally feared by some, it is irrationally welcomed by others. Disorganization—chaos—the "mindless explosion" of repressed rage: all are welcomed, mistaken for a liberating of the deepest soul.

ROBERT PENN WARREN

The Enunciation of Universality

"The Zodiac," by James Dickey, is a poem in twelve parts, a major undertaking and, I should hazard, achievement. According to a headnote, it is based on another poem of the same title, written by a Dutchman, one Hendrik Marsman, who was killed by a torpedo in the North Atlantic in 1940. But, the headnote asserts, this is no mere translation, for only a few lines are drawn from the original. And the reader can easily understand how Dickey's temperament would have led him to relive and rewrite and, in the process, transform Marsman's poem.

The central character, and for the most part the spokesman direct or indirect, of the poem, the son of an amateur astronomer, is an alcoholic, perhaps dying—a wanderer, a *deraciné* poet, who after years of alienation has returned to Holland, which

                                                    is good enough
    To die in. That's the place to lay down
    His screwed-up body-meat. That's it.
                                This is it.
    It's that thing you might call home.

In Amsterdam, in a lonely room at the head of rickety stairs, full of rhetoric and imagery and aquavit, the wanderer seeks in a final desperation to establish some relation with the world, sometimes by musing on his fouled-up life but basically, as the son of the astronomer father, by a mys-

From *New York Times Book Review* (November 14, 1976). ©1976 by the New York Times Co.

tique of the stars of his revised and redemptive Zodiac. The main sections
occur at night in a little upper room:

> The town square below, deserted as a Siberian crater, lies in the middle
> Of his white-writing darkness   stroboscoped   red-stopped by the
>   stammering mess
>   Of the city's unbombed neon, sent through rivers and many cities
>   By fourth-class mail from Hell.

With daylight, in section 9, the poet wanders forth to meet old places,
old memories, including those of early love ("*The* grave *of* youth? HA! *I
told you:* There's nobody *in* it!"), and with "his forehead on the stone-
grains of the wall," an ivied wall, he hears his mother's voice:

> "Never come back here.
>   Don't wander around your own youth.
>   Time is too painful here. Nothing stays with you
>   But what you remember. The memory-animal crouched
> Head-down   a huge lizard   in these vines, sleeping like winter,
> Wrapped in dead leaves, lifts its eyes and pulls its lips back
>   Only at reunion."

Later, back in his room, he is visited by a young woman, but in the
twilight

>   he knows that nothing,
>   Even love, can kill off his lonesomeness.

and dawn finds their souls

>   Fallen from them, left in the night
>   Of patterns   the night that's just finished
>   Overwhelming the earth.

with its undecipherable pattern of stars.
   So he returns to thoughts of his wanderings and his obsessions with
poetry and stars while

>   The darkness stretched out on the waters
>   Pulls back, humming Genesis.

So much for the frame of the poem, which is consistently demanding,
characteristically eloquent and often in an original way, and sometimes
magnificent. I can think of no poem since Hart Crane's "The Bridge" that
is so stylistically ambitious and has aimed to stir such depths of emotion.

Like "The Bridge" (and most works of man's hand) this poem has certain limitations and defects that may provoke quarrel: for instance, the structural principle of progression for the first seven or eight sections is not always clear, and there is again some sort of structural blockage in the last two sections—defects in, we may say, the dramatic pivots. But the audacity of imagery, assemblage of rhythms, the power of language redeems all—in a period too often marked by a delicate hovering over the fragile merely because it is fragile and the prosy because it is prosy, the celebration of sensibility as such, polite or academic scrupulosities, self-pity in a cruel world, craven free verse lacking basic and projective rhythms.

In one sense "The Zodiac" can be said to be about the over-ambitiousness of poetry—even as it celebrates its ambitiousness. Even as the drunk poet stares at the stars, he says

> they are pictures
> Of some sort of meaning. He thinks the secret
> Can be read.

Or:

> But by God we've got a universe
> Here
> Those designs of time are saying something.

Poetry, for the drunk poet as for Crane, is the enunciation of universality. The question is double. First, is it true only of the *drunk* poet? Second, is there *in vino veritas*? Then we must ask, what kind of *veritas*? The poem is a metaphysical poem, one that with passion, rage, eloquence, and occasionally hysterical yammer asks a metaphysical question as a form of poetry. If for nothing, it would be memorable for the passage that seals the end:

> But now, *now*
> Oh God you rocky landscape   give me,   Give
> Me drop by drop
> desert water at least.
> I want now to write about deserts
>
> And in the dark the sand begins to cry
> For living water that not a sun or star
> Can kill, and for the splay camel-prints that bring men,
> And the ocean with its enormous crooning, begs

For haunted sailors   for refugees putting back
  Flesh on their ever-tumbling bones
   To man that fleet,
         for in its ships
    Only, the sea becomes the sea.

Oh my own soul, put me in a solar boat.
  Come into one of these hands
  Bringing quietness and the rare belief
That I can steer this strange craft to the morning
Land that sleeps   in the universe on all horizons
· · · · · · · · · · · · · · · · ·

So long as the spirit hurls on space
The star-beasts of intellect and madness.

LINDA WAGNER

Deliverance: *Initiation and Possibility*

For all his collections of poetry, James Dickey came closest to capturing his personal mythopoeic vision in the controversial novel *Deliverance*. That his vision was admittedly masculine seems unnecessary to justify, and that the novel was filled with violence, gore, and sport imagery is also defensible. For what Dickey was creating in his novel was a *Pilgrim's Progress* of male egoism, complete with all varieties of masculine fantasy—physical power and prowess, sexual expectation and satisfaction, and above all, contest, competition. What he achieved in the execution of the novel was a resolution far different from his characters' expectations—whether those of Lewis Medlock, the greatest achiever, or those of Ed Gentry, the follower. Dickey's resolution was an understanding beyond fantasy, an understanding of the reality of life, and an acceptance.

In his story of initiation and ritual, initiation through ritual, Dickey balances the characters' expectations before the canoeing trip with their recognition of reality after it. For emphasis, he divides the novel into five sections, the first titled simply "Before," the last, "After"; the three middle sections carry the dates of the three days of the trip, September 14, 15, and 16. Each of the five segments has its particular progression, both as part of the continuum of the book and as its own unit; the ending of each is especially significant. "Before" ends with Ed viewing the young golden-eyed model as some kind of nymph (he speaks of a "deep and complex male thrill" as he watches her), her golden eye "more gold than any real gold could possibly be; it was alive." She represents the possibility of his return-

From *The South Carolina Review* 10, no. 2 (April 1978). © 1978 by Linda Wagner.

ing to youth and energy: the fear of aging, death, permeates the "Before" section:

> The feeling of the inconsequence of whatever I would do, of anything I would pick up or think about or turn to see was at that moment being set in the very bone marrow. How does one get through this? I asked myself. . . . It was the old mortal, helpless, time-terrified human feeling.

One mark of this fear of mortality is the men's need to merge with nature and its beings. Ed notes with pleasure, "I sat with the pressure of the woods against me; when I looked down I saw that one leaf was shaking with my heart." By the end of "September 14," Ed finds his imaginative fulfillment in his interlude with the mysterious owl, who with its claws tears through the tent where he and Drew are sleeping. Just as Ed had touched the girl at the close of the first section, so now he touches the owl: "I slipped my forefinger between the claw and the tent, and half around the stony toe. The claw tightened." Taking his identity from the bird, Ed then "hunted with him as well as I could, there in my weightlessness. The woods burned in my head." Union complete, Ed—and his friends—revel in the communion with nature. As the quiet Drew remarked, "I've always wanted to do this. . . . Only I didn't know it."

The euphoric mood changes at the beginning of "September 15," however, when Ed slips into his fog-colored long underwear to merge with the atmosphere, for the purpose of killing a deer, and misses the animal through human failure, buck fever. Soon Ed and Bobby are captured, Bobby raped, Lewis a murderer, and Drew killed. At the close of "September 15," Ed is wedged inhumanly in a rock crevice "like a lizard," his quest no longer a romantic tryst with nature. His mission at the close of the second day is a simple search for revenge and self-preservation, through the execution of still another murder. Hunted, man will also hunt: "The world is easily lost."

The close of "September 16" brings the image of Ed, bloodied and sodden after one of the longest days in contemporary American fiction, cognizant that his body is dry, so dry, standing half asleep under the river-water shower in the blue-green light of the basement. But when he goes upstairs, to bed, there is no transformation: he remains himself. There is no fusion with any other sort of being or consciousness, memory or fantasy. All that is left is the reality. "It was over. I lay awake all night in the brilliant sleep." The glory that had previously come only through imagined exploits, the gold that had spun its color only from unattainable images, was now a part of Ed's common experience of human renewal.

The closing sections bring Ed back to his reverence for the river ("The river and everything I remembered about it became a possession to me, a personal, private possession, as nothing else in my life ever had. Now it ran nowhere but in my head, but there it ran as though immortally. . . . In me it still is, and will be until I die, green, rocky, deep, fast, slow, and beautiful beyond reality"), a reverence that is incorruptible, for the water is ageless, timeless, pure. It is the human factor that corrupts, and only the human factor.

Once into the "After" segment, Dickey makes it eminently clear that Lewis and Ed have learned from their experience, have come full circle to an appreciation of the reality of their lives. They dare very little that is foolhardy. They settle, as it were, near another lake, sharing their knowledge and their severely limited power. It is all so different from the opening scene and their expectations; and that great, and grave, difference is the point of *Deliverance:* the *doing* is the knowledge. Only in the doing, when bared to the essential, the zero at the bone, does a person come to know himself. Playing against the overbearing male pride so evident in the opening passage, Dickey chooses his epigrams for the novel to stress the vanity of pride—in self, strength, control. The real control, as Lewis comes to observe, may lie in losing it. But in the opening scene, every word works hard to emphasize the power and control in Lewis's hands:

> It unrolled slowly, forced to show its colors, curling and snapping back whenever one of us turned loose. The whole land was very tense until we put our four steins on its corners and laid the river out to run for us through the mountains 150 miles north. Lewis' hand took a pencil and marked out a small strong X in a place where some of the green bled away and the paper changed with high ground, and began to work downstream, northeast to southwest through the printed woods. I watched the hand rather than the location, for it seemed to have power over the terrain, and when it stopped for Lewis' voice to explain something, it was as though all streams everywhere quit running, hanging silently where they were to let the point be made.

The human control of "the whole land," caught and tamed under beer steins; the power of Lewis's hand and voice—Dickey's image of the living map as land evokes vividly the theme of the novel, man's belief in his physical power to control. (Lewis touts the studied development of his body; the four men are each conscious of their naked appearances.) The tone of the active verbs, however, darkens the image, suggesting rape through

the words *forced* and *bled away,* and the figure of the land (usually feminine) being *unrolled,* then *curling, snapping,* is also suggestive. The physi-
cality of the men's force is emphasized too in the dehumanization of "Lewis's
hand," acting as if without conscious direction in its "small strong" mark.
The unidentified pronoun *It* also suggests more than the simple scene that is
actually described.

The passage also opens the pervading color imagery—the kindly green
bleeds away; the threat of omnipresent blue; the implication of ruin in the
red of the verb *bled.* Later, Dickey begins the use of the evanescent gold, first
in the more-than-real gold of the woman's eyes; then in the "light green-
gold" of the developing leaves; finally the magical green becoming his identity: "I was light green, a tall forest man, an explorer, guerrilla, hunter."
The most noticeable detail about Dickey's use of color imagery is its absence
once the sodomy scene begins: from then on the only emphasized color is
the red of the wasted blood, first on his own chest, then "like an apple" in
the dying man's mouth, finally in a ferocious flood with Ed's murder of the
second victim:

> The top of his chest was another color, and as he melted forward
> and down I saw the arrow hanging down his back just below the
> neck; it was painted entirely red, and was just hanging by the
> nock and flipping stiffly and softly. He got carefully down to his
> knees; blood poured when his mouth opened and seemed to
> splash up out of the ground, to have the force of something
> coming out of the earth, a spring revealed when the right stone
> was moved. Die, I thought, my God, die, die.

All the attempts at evasion—not describing the "color" of the opening line,
giving the arrow's presence an innocence and softness that changed its real
role, trying to imply a naturalness to the man's bleeding to death—cannot
counteract Ed's recognition of his responsibility that the last sentence reveals. But the handling of the blood image, and the omission of the color
red, makes this an unusually powerful description.

Incremental in this scene, which includes Ed's own arrow wound and
its removal, the haze of blood shrouds the action as well as the scene: Ed
must follow the dying man by his bloody trail, covering that blood, as he
moves, with his own. After this scene, all gold is gone from the novel, except
for the yellow tree, symbol of the collective and staining lie; but that color
does not pretend to gold. Only the natural green and the darkness of the
river remain.

Dickey's color imagery comes to suggest the dichotomy between fantasy and reality. For all the talk about fantasy ("That's all anybody has got. It depends on how strong your fantasy is, and whether you really—*really*—in your own mind, fit into your own fantasy, whether you measure up to what you've fantasized"), Lewis and Ed both know, finally, that reality is their final power: "I believe in survival. All kinds. . . . I am becoming myself, as inconsequential as that may be. I am not something somebody shoved off on me. I am what I choose to be, and I am *it*." Lewis's pride in self-knowledge is premature, however, and just as wrong as Ed's belief that only through the imaginative, the unreal, the mysterious image of the golden-eyed girl in the midst of making love to Martha could he find what he needed ("another life, deliverance"). Through characterization, imagery, and structure, Dickey makes, and remakes, his points.

Perhaps the chief weakness in *Deliverance* is the fact that all its parts do mesh so well. The explicit leads of the opening—with the charged dialogue between Ed and Lewis, even though it may be ironic dialogue, speech that we as readers understand as naive and indulgent—leave very little for the reader to come to alone. Once into the story, however, the demands of the plot keep Dickey from repeating his theme excessively; the movement of the book is apt for this twentieth-century river story. Dickey's is an incremental yet never leisurely rhythm, based on moderately long sentences which often branch with unexpected modifiers, and come up short in a simpler structure. The shorter sentence often repeats a key element from the longer:

> With my cheek on one shoulder, I lay there on my side in the crevice, facing out, not thinking about anything, solid on one side with stone and open to the darkness on the other, as though I were in a sideways grave. The glass of the bow was cold in my hands, cold and familiar. The curves were beautiful to the touch, a smooth chill flowing, and beside the curves the arrow lay—or stood—rigidly, the feathers bristling when I moved a little, and the points pricking at me. But it was good pain; it was reality, and deep in the situation.

The voice of Ed Gentry, narrator, not unlike Dickey's own in poems like "Driving" and "Falling," maintains its pace, suiting its narrative to the natural flow of the action. Dickey-Gentry is good at controlling not only what the reader learns, but the manner in which he learns it. In this scene with a change of movement, as the hunted man realizes danger is near, Dickey varies the tempo of the sentences to build suspense:

> I was down to my last two points, and he was still right there,
> stooping a little but now facing me just a shade more than he had
> been. Then he moved, slightly but quickly, and I fought to hold
> on to the arrow. He stirred the ground once with his foot, and I
> saw his face—saw that he had a face—for the first time. The
> whole careful structure of my shot began to come apart, and I
> struggled in my muscles and guts and heart to hold it together.
> His eyes were moving over the sand and rock, faster and faster.
> They were coming.

The masterful parenthetical "saw that he had a face," which personalizes
the encounter tremendously, stops the action briefly before Dickey resumes
the intense pace. Because of writing like this, the similarity of much of the
narrative—long accounts of action in the river, or in the hunt—never becomes repetitious.

Viewed as a masculine initiation story, set on a river, *Deliverance* can
be considered a kind of gothic, even bitter, *Adventures of Huckleberry Finn.*
That the story is no idyll is part of Dickey's theme: the simple tests, the
primitive encounters, may be almost beyond civilized people—not out of
their own deficiency, either physical or moral—but from the exigencies of
common sense. Just as Dickey's comments on the seemingly pastoral life are
scathing in their satire, and the doctor echoes them, so his notion that
civilization *has* brought humanity pervades the "After" section. His experience has brought him new strength in his own minor art; he adds to his
friends; he has recognized that Drew, in his understanding of and ability to
play music, and to believe in morality, was the strongest of them all. Tom
Sawyer relinquished his fantasy, or at least Huck Finn did. So too did Ed
and Lewis (but Bobby, in contrast, searched only further and further, finally
going, so people said, to Hawaii). And the "deliverance" that Ed expected
to find in some imaginative escape was finally to be his not by leaving
reality, but by immersing himself in it.

> I went downtown. The main thing was to get back into my life
> as quickly and as deeply as I could; as if I had never left it. I
> walked into my office and opened the door wide so that anybody
> who wanted to look could see me there, shuffling papers and
> layouts.

There are other borrowings—partly satiric, partly poignant—from
Twain, especially from *Huck:* the gold imagery, suggesting first the treasure
and then the piles of gold in Huck's imagination, gold which, at the close of

his novel, Huck is ready to give to Tom, if only he can leave the Widow Douglas. The search for freedom, Huck's ideal, about which Ed wonders on September 15, "Is this freedom?" Huck's use of the truth-lie imagery ("I never seen anybody but lied one time or another"), which becomes the moral center of *Deliverance*. Huck's yearning for his "old rags," rags that Ed finally gives up to be burned, and for blood, this aplenty in Ed's far-from-romantic experience. There are also owls, "who-whooing about some-body that was dead," owls in *Deliverance* who return to Dean's tent the night before his death; conspiratorial friendships, considerably darker in the adult context Dickey gives them; and a plain and simple wanderlust:

> All I wanted was to go somewheres; all I wanted was a change,
> I warn't particular.

The wisdom of *Deliverance* is that this Huck-like quest, without purpose or direction, is shown to be futile. "How come? How come you to be doing this, in the fust place?" the skeptical inlanders ask Ed. And there is, of course, no answer: "Oh," I said, hesitating and not really knowing the answer, even now. "I guess we just wanted to get out a little."

Reminiscent of Twain too is the important relationship between Lewis and Ed, a hero-worship situation at the beginning, based on Lewis's physical prowess and daring, become by the end of the novel a recognition between equals, a shift of power not unlike that between Tom Sawyer and Huck. Tom's rhetoric in his case, the "right" way to adventure, to dare, was Lewis's "All-American" myth, male as muscle-building, sexually-prowling animal, predator known by his feats of strength and conquest, of whatever kind. Just as Huck's innocent and incisive acts topple Tom Sawyer's reliance on literary ritual, so the horrifying events of the real wilderness life (not that of villagers playing dulcimers) destroy the modern men's expectations—and it is particularly, if grotesquely, appropriate that, since so much of this kind of male identity is located in sexual prowess, here sodomy is the means to the men's initiation.

The sodomy is also the cause of the first murder, as Lewis reacts in a typically masculine pattern when he kills for the crime (that Bobby's "injury" turns out to be minor compared to those of the other three is another ironic comment on the impact of the situation). Only Drew questions the validity of Lewis's murder; only Drew has, this early in the novel, accepted his responsibility, its pain and its rewards. That acceptance is to be the deliverance of both Lewis and Ed, and their lives show their maturity in living them. Ed has new relationships, continued love for Martha, satisfaction from his son Dean. And Lewis "limps over from his cabin now and then and we look at each other with intelligence, feeling the true weight and purpose of all water. He has changed, too, but not in obvious ways. He can die now; he knows that dying is better than immortality. He is a human being, and a good one."

The three days of Dickey's *Deliverance* have seemed like an eternity, and in some ways they are. But they give Ed, and Lewis, and perhaps Dickey himself, the kind of freedom from the stereotyped male image, and from the pride, that blinds so many would-be powerful men. It is no simple journey; rather it is a contemporary descent into hell, modeled on the exploration-of-self through exploration-of-river that images a peculiarly American, masculine quest for identity:

> Why on God's earth am I here? I thought. . . . Something or other was being made good. I touched the knife hilt at my side, and remembered that all men were once boys, and that boys are always looking for ways to become men.

NEAL BOWERS

Selling the Poem

No one in this century has talked and written more about his poetry and his poetics than has James Dickey. In this respect, he has been the ultimate pitchman. The fear that saying too much about the creative process might somehow weaken or destroy it, an abiding neurosis of many contemporary poets, appears not to bother Dickey. In fact, he seems to fuel his creative drive by responding at length to questions put to him, no matter how trivial they may sound or how repetitive they may have become over the years. Consequently, we know a great deal about how Dickey works and what he hopes to accomplish in his poetry. We have, for example, his claim that he writes all the time, even in his sleep, and that he considers himself "one of those slow, plodding, searching writers" [*Self-Interviews;* all further references to this text will be abbreviated as *SI*]. We know that he revises laboriously and always has three or four different things in progress simultaneously, in different typewriters scattered around his house.

Dickey talks about these things because they are mysterious and interesting to him. Like the man who can move small objects without touching them and without knowing how he does it, Dickey is as intrigued by his own creative powers as outside observers are. All his talk reflects a person trying to understand the poetic process himself, not a writer who has reduced everything to convenient formulas. This attitude explains in part why Dickey would be interested in interviewing himself or in telling everything he knows about the origin and writing of a poem. Beyond the obvious and much

From *James Dickey: The Poet as Pitchman.* © 1985 by the Curators of the University of Missouri. The University of Missouri Press, 1985.

criticized jungle of egocentrism lies a surprisingly large lake of objectivity and simple curiosity.

The problem for the reader wishing to follow Dickey's self-analysis is basically one of abundance. There is so much material that it is difficult to know where to begin. Luckily, Dickey is remarkably consistent in his poetic philosophy, even to the point of being repetitive, and that helps to make things more manageable. Of particular interest to this study is a remark Dickey made about his earliest poetry, one he has stood by through all the changes in his subsequent work: "I wanted immediacy, the effect of spontaneity, and reader involvement more than anything else. I also wanted to see if I could work with narrative elements in new and maybe peculiar ways" (*SI*). If an entire career can be summarized in such a small space, these two statements tell the whole story of his poetic endeavor: the desire for reader involvement and the attempts to effect it through narrative experimentation.

At a Dickey reading, there has never been any question that the audience would become involved in the performance of the poetry, thanks largely to Dickey's engaging presence. But Dickey is talking here about participation for the reader rather than the auditor. Borrowing a term from Alfred North Whitehead, Dickey says that he is after "presentational immediacy," but not in an oral sense:

> No, I don't mean the presentation, say, from a reading platform. I mean, for words to come together into some kind of magical conjunction that will make the reader enter into a real experience of his own—*not* the poet's. I don't really believe what literary critics have believed from the beginning of time: that poetry is an attempt of the poet to create or recreate his own experience and to pass it on. I don't believe in that. I believe it's an awakening of the sensibilities of someone else, the stranger.
>
> (*Night Hurdling*)

These observations about the reader and his relationship to the created work clearly place Dickey with the phenomenologists. He is more interested in the affective possibilities of his poetry and in the reader's ability to respond to that poetry in an individual and private way than in handing over a parcel containing his own attitudes and emotions. According to Dickey, the poetic exchange ought to produce "an awakening of the sensibility of someone else. It's giving *his* experience to *him*. It's revitalizing his experience, rather than trying to pass yours on to him" (*Night Hurdling*).

It is not clear whether Dickey would go so far as to say the work itself is secondary to the reader's response, existing only in the reader's consciousness. He approaches analysis of his own poetry with the eye of a New Critic, saying all the while, "I'm not trying to impose an official interpretation on the poems; that would be the last thing I would want to do. As one reader of my verse and as the person who happened to create the poems, I offer the following remarks for whatever interest they have to people who want to look at the poems from my standpoint as well as their own" (*SI*). Significantly, Dickey regards himself as "one reader" of his poetry among many probable readers, all presumably capable of responding in their own ways, regardless of what Dickey may have to say. But unlike the true New Critic, who would disallow the poet's comments on his own work on the grounds of the intentional fallacy, Dickey insists on his right to be affected by what he has written and to talk about how he as a reader receives the poems.

If "presentational immediacy" is the objective, narrative is the technique Dickey employs to attain it. Curiously, though, some critics have failed to acknowledge Dickey as a narrative poet. Paul Ramsey, for example, has identified Dickey as a failed lyric poet, saying, "a great lyric rhythm found him; he varied it, loosened it, then left it, to try an inferior form." In reality, a very different process occurred: Dickey had a brief, early flirtation with the lyric, during which time he was embarrassingly derivative, but he soon discovered his true power and originality in the narrative, which, as a staple of English and American poetry, is far from being an inferior form. To see just how unformed Dickey was as a lyric poet, one needs only to look at some passages from his first book, *Into the Stone* (1960). There we find echoes of Dylan Thomas:

> Nor rise, nor shine, nor live
> With any but the slant, green, mummied light
> And wintry, bell-swung undergloom of waters
> > (*Poems*)

the voice of Hopkins made thin through anapests:

> Now, owing my arms to the dead
> Tree, and the leaf-loosing, mortal wood,
> Still hearing that music amaze me,
> I walk through the time-stricken forest
> > (*Poems*)

and Roethke unabashedly cribbed:

The dead have their chance in my body.
The stars are drawn into their myths.
I bear nothing but moonlight upon me.
I am known; I know my love.

(*Poems*)

The most memorable poem in that first volume is "The Performance," and it is not merely coincidental that the poem is a strong narrative. For Dickey, finding his own true voice coincided with discovering the narrative and working less with the lyric. What he wanted was the poetry of participation rather than of reflection, and he found it and the possibility for increased reader involvement in the narrative (*Sorties*).

This, then, is how Dickey sells the poem, by using narrative techniques and involving the reader in some kind of action. In Dickey's own words, he "wants, more than anything else, for the poem to be an experience—that is, a *physical* experience—for the reader. It must be a completed action, and the plunging in of the reader into this action is the most difficult and the most desirable feat that the poet can perform" (*Sorties*). To achieve the effects Dickey wants most, the reader must be pulled into a dramatic situation. The lyric confronts the reader with reflection, but the narrative tells a story and beckons the reader to become involved with the action of that story. In this respect, Dickey has said that his work "attempts to win back for poetry some of the territory that poetry has unnecessarily relinquished to the novel" (*Sorties*).

Having taken the position that he wanted for "most of [his] poems . . . a sense of *story*" (*Sorties*), Dickey soon discovered great flexibility in the narrative form. Perhaps he oversimplified things in identifying only two basic ways to present a story: "One way is for the story to be obvious; that is, for there to be a beginning, middle, and end in that order. The other way is for the story to be implicit, and there are a million ways of doing this" (*Sorties*). But even such a generalization shows how much potential he saw in the story poem. The poetry itself reveals a growing fascination with style and diction and their connection to point of view. The range reaches all the way from a standard narrative like "The Performance," to the first-person delivery of a sermon by a woman preacher, to the third-person accounts of what an airline stewardess's fall from an airplane might have been like and what a drunken, half-crazy Dutch poet determined to fix his position in the universe might think and say, to a woman's girlhood "male-imagined."

Dickey's growing interest in the narrative poem coincided with his starting to work on *Deliverance* in 1962. But if the novel in progress influenced his poetry, his poetry impacted on the novel, so much so that Dickey's final revisions of *Deliverance* were undertaken to stress "a straightforward novel more and the poetic aspects of a lyrical novel less." The struggle to find some point of balance between lyric and narrative is central to Dickey's work, and though he has remained committed to the lyric, his poems succeed in almost direct proportion to their narrative content. That is why *Puella* (1982) disappoints: the narrative has been subordinated to the lyric.

The effort to reconcile narrative and lyric is clearly evident in several poems in Dickey's first book, *Into the Stone* (1960), but nowhere more so than in "Sleeping Out at Easter," which opens with this stanza:

> All dark is now no more.
> This forest is drawing a light.
> All Presences change into trees.
> One eye opens slowly without me.
> My sight is the same as the sun's,
> For this is the grave of the king,
> Where the earth turns, waking a choir.
> *All dark is now no more.*
>
> (*Poems*)

In his comments on this poem, Dickey has said that he told himself before writing it to "Make it immediate. Put the reader and yourself *in medias res,* in the middle of an action" (*SI*). The emphasis is on the narrative, as Dickey's use of the term *in medias res,* which describes the conventional opening of an epic poem, suggests. So we begin by waking somewhere with the speaker, apparently outside among trees. The title, of course, has already tipped us off to this; but still, the narrative engages us in a process of discovery as we come to see a man waking at dawn in his own back yard after a night of sleeping out. His wife, beginning to stir inside the house, sees him through a window; his child sleeps on, mystically feeling the significance of this situation.

Dickey himself sees two things in this poem. First, there is the story, which is "just about a man sleeping in back of his house and becoming another person on Easter through the twin influences of the Easter ritual and of nature itself. His rebirth is symbolized by nothing more or less than waking up in a strange place which is near a familiar place" (*SI*). So much for the narrative component.

But Dickey also sees something mysterious in the poem, something that goes beyond the simple telling of a story, and that quality is communicated through lines with a "marked rhythmical effect," "an almost hypnotic beat"

(*SI*). This is the purely lyrical aspect of the poem, which is represented best by the final stanza, a combination of lines taken from throughout the poem and offered as a kind of coda:

> *All dark is now no more.*
> *In your palm is the secret of waking.*
> *Put down those seeds in your hand;*
> *All Presences change into trees.*
> *A feather shall drift from the pine-top.*
> *The sun shall have told you this song,*
> *For this is the grave of the king;*
> *For the king's grave turns you to light.*
>
> (*Poems*)

Gathered as they are at the end, and italicized to suggest a greater significance, these lines stand as a lyrical comment on the narrative aspect of the poem. It is curious that Dickey felt, at least at this early point in his career, that the narrative could not carry the theme and suggest something of mystery on its own. Though it may be an interesting experiment, the poem has a heavy-handedness that keeps it from working as well as Dickey wanted it to. However caught up in the immediacy of the narrative readers might be, they are likely to lose interest by the end of the poem, when the narrator is pushed aside by the intrusive poet intent on resonating something mysterious.

By way of contrast, "The Performance" shows where Dickey's true powers lie, in a forceful narrative presentation. The immediacy Dickey hoped for in "Sleeping Out at Easter" is fully realized here, as the reader is swept up by the narrative voice from the very first statement:

> The last time I saw Donald Armstrong
> He was staggering oddly off into the sun,
> Going down, of the Philippine Islands.
>
> (*Poems*)

Using a traditional narrative opening, which begins at the beginning rather than in the middle of things, Dickey's narrator immediately engages the reader with an evocative recollection of someone named Donald Armstrong. The locale, the Philippines, the simple assertion that this is a memory of seeing Armstrong for the last time, the ambiguous possibilities of the word "staggering," and the symbolic potential of Armstrong's movement into the setting sun all help to create an intriguing dramatic situation that draws the reader into the poem to discover more. What the reader learns is that

Armstrong was in the Philippines during the war, that he was staggering because he was walking on his hands, and that he was killed by his Japanese captors the day after the speaker saw him looming precariously upside-down in the sunset.

Though it is arguable that "The Performance" is more interesting than "Sleeping Out at Easter" simply because of its subject matter, the effectiveness of each poem is largely determined by how its content is presented. While the speaker of "Sleeping Out at Easter" talks or thinks to himself in short sentences and end-stopped lines, the voice in "The Performance" directly addresses the reader in a more natural, conversational way. Accounting for this difference by saying it reflects the difference between lyric and narrative poetry may be tempting, but it does not accurately explain what distinguishes these two poems from one another. After all, "Sleeping Out at Easter" is a narrative, even though it resolves itself into pure lyric at the end; and "The Performance" certainly contains lyrical passages, such as the following:

> Standing there on his hands,
> On his spindle-shanked forearms balanced,
> Unbalanced, with his big feet looming and waving
> In the great, untrustworthy air
> He flew in each night, when it darkened.
>
> (*Poems*)

This passage more than holds its own alongside "My child, mouth open, still sleeping, / Hears the song in the egg of a bird" (*Poems*), the statement in "Sleeping Out at Easter" that Dickey finds filled with such resonance and mystery. What finally separates these two poems and makes them so different is Dickey's attitude. In the Easter poem, he strains after significance and ends by imposing mystery and meaning on the situation. But in remembering Donald Armstrong, he simply tells the story and lets the details body forth whatever significance they may have.

Dickey's attitude, or his poetic stance, impinges upon everything he has written and accounts for how the poet who could write a moving, troubling poem like "The Firebombing" could also write "The Poisoned Man" with its excess allegorical baggage. When Dickey trusts in his material and in his ability to order detail in the most evocative way, he is an exceptional poet. But when he gives his material a booster injection of meaning and significance he can be as tedious as Robert Service or as didactic as Edgar Guest. In his drive to find what he calls the "glory," Dickey has always been drawn to the lyrical, to the magical, incantatory qualities inherent in language. In fact, Dickey's more recent poetry (such as that in *Puella*) reveals an almost total commitment to the lyrical. This is a lamentable but perhaps inevitable defection from the narrative camp, the result of a career-long struggle to accommodate a lyrical impulse within the scope of a narrative gift.

It was Dickey's narrative poetry, however, that accounted in large part for his popularity during the 1960s, for his success in "selling" his work. Within the narrative poem, Dickey discovered a range of rhetorical strategies associated with the speaker's voice: repetition, mixed diction (formal with colloquial), and a complex sentence structure that allows the poem to gather speed and pull the reader along toward the syntactical and thematic climax. These techniques disarm, perhaps even mesmerize, and involve the reader as much as possible in the poem. Just as Dickey's voice and manner at the podium captured an audience, the voices speaking from the printed page invite the reader to participate fully in the poem. They may take on the tone of friend, confessor, carnival barker, or evangelical preacher, but all are designed to sell the poem by catching the reader up in it.

"The Performance" exemplifies Dickey's early efforts in what he called "mythologizing my own factual experience" (*SI*). Extrapolating from the actual capture and decapitation of a fellow pilot named Donald Armstrong, Dickey imagines what his friend might have done before the sword fell. Because "you can make anything you like happen in a poem," he has Armstrong perform his acrobatics before kneeling down to be beheaded (*SI*). The true potential of the subject matter is realized in the poem through what Dickey calls "the creative possibilities of the lie" (*SI*). In Dickey's view, the poet "comes to understand that he is not after the 'truth' at all but something that he considers better. He understands that he is not trying to tell the truth but to *make* it, so that the vision of the poem will impose itself on the reader as more memorable and value-laden than the actuality it is taken from" (*Sorties*). Of course, this kind of fabricating is the heart of fiction, and as an element essential to Dickey's poetic narratives it represents another way in which the reader's attention can be gained and held.

The only serious problem with pursuit of a truth better than truth is that it sometimes tends toward abstraction, as in the title poem of *Into the Stone*. Even if Dickey had not said so, we would have no trouble guessing that the poem has no factual context but is based instead on "a vague idea about the quality of a love relationship, especially in its early stages when it changes the world for the person in love" (*SI*). Here, as in "Sleeping Out at Easter," Dickey is lured by the lyric as by the Siren's call, and he ends up on the rocks rather than moving "into the stone." The title itself reflects the terribly abstract nature of the poem, especially since Dickey never makes it clear what the stone might be or how it is possible to move into it. For help with such puzzles we have only the line "Through the stone held in air by my heartbeat" (*Poems*). Whatever lyrical qualities this line may possess are more than offset by its obscurity. But here, as in "Sleeping Out at Easter," Dickey is principally interested in the mysterious qualities he can evoke through language. The lines are mostly end-stopped; the rhythm is either hypnotic (as Dickey would have it) or monotonous; and the man and woman are incorporeal. Had Dickey written only poems of this type, his books would never have been dog-eared and few people would have turned out to hear him read, even on a mild night in spring.

"The Lifeguard" is another poem that begins in the middle of things; unlike "Into the Stone," however, it offers a real character instead of a wispy shape in the moonlight. The speaker finds himself in the most human of situations, wishing to undo a tragic occurrence. When the poem opens, we find him in a boathouse at night, "From all sleeping children hidden" (*Poems*). The dramatic situation created by this setting leads to speculation about the identity of the speaker and why he is hiding from the children. As curiosity draws us further into the poem, the speaker does something impossible:

> I rise and go out through the boats.
> I set my broad sole upon silver,
> On the skin of the sky, on the moonlight,
> Stepping outward from earth onto water
> In quest of the miracle
>
> This village of children believed
> That I could perform as I dived
> For one who had sunk from my sight.
> I saw his cropped haircut go under.
> I leapt, and my steep body flashed
> Once, in the sun.
>
> (*Poems*)

He is either walking on water or imagining himself to be, but however we read the poem we find ourselves, by this point, involved in an extraordinary narrative. The mood is not quasi-mythical, as in "Sleeping Out at Easter," or abstract-ethereal as in "Into the Stone," but true beyond the possibility of truth. Confronted with the implacability and the irreversibility of death, the lifeguard can only fantasize or actually perform a miracle. Nothing less will do. To save a child who is beyond saving, he must become Christ-like and resurrect him from the moon-illumined lake.

The poem, then, represents the psychological stages in coming to terms with grief and, in this case, its attendant guilt. Having failed in his duty to protect the children swimming at the summer camp, the lifeguard withdraws from reality. His initial impulse is to hide from the truth and from his failure to save the drowning child. The second stage is to wish for the power to undo the death, and so he imagines himself walking across the lake to reclaim the lost boy. Both tactics, evasion and hallucination, finally give way to a confrontation of reality and an acceptance of the situation as the lifeguard washes the mud from his hands, symbolically absolving himself of guilt, having done all he could humanly do. He then turns his attention from himself to the child, for whom he is finally able to grieve.

Though "The Lifeguard" is not based on autobiographical fact, as is "The Performance," it is equally true. The specific character and the dramatic situation enable Dickey, or perhaps empower him, to create truth; and the poem succeeds to the extent that he is able to project himself into the character of the lifeguard and experience his predicament. The process of assuming a persona is central to what Dickey calls the fiction of the poem and involves answering some fundamental questions:

> The questions he must answer in this respect come to the poet in forms not so much like "What did I do then?" but rather "What might I have done?" or "What would it be interesting for me to do, given the situation as I am giving it?" Or perhaps, if the poet is prone to speak in this way, "What can I make my agent do that will truly *find* the poem: that will focus it on or around a human action and deliver a sense of finality and consequence, and maybe even that aura of strangeness that Bacon said every 'excellent beauty' must possess?"
>
> (*Sorties*)

In other words, the poet does not discover a character and then search for things he might already have done. Instead, the poet and his character mutually inhabit one another and together create the facts of the poem. The process for Dickey involves vigorously pushing at the limits of credibility to make the persona do something truly memorable and, with luck, to discover "that aura of strangeness."

Even the casual reader of Dickey's poetry immediately recognizes the quality of strangeness Dickey values so greatly. It is there in the brightening yard of a man sleeping outside at Easter, in the joyous, perfect acrobatics of a soldier about to be executed, and in the lifeguard's first step "from earth onto water." This fascination with the eerie, the bizarre, and even the grotesque is a hallmark of Dickey's work and has been one of the reasons for its appeal. One is not likely to encounter in the work of any other poet a sheep child speaking from a bottle of alcohol, an airline stewardess disrobing as she falls to her death, or a railroad bum becoming a celebrity after being nailed to the side of a boxcar. So strong is Dickey's attraction to the unusual that his poetry often tends toward surrealism, though it usually maintains touch, however tenuously, with reality. According to Dickey, "The poem should come of reality and go back into it. But it should *impose* itself on fact" (*Sorties*). Certainly, that is what happens in "The Lifeguard," as we move from the speaker's attempt to hide, through his fantasy of resurrecting the drowned child, and finally to his acceptance of grief.

In great part, Dickey's popularity has been the product of his willingness (at times, even his eagerness) to take chances. He is the high-wire performer who draws in the crowd not simply because he balances sixty feet up without a net but because he keeps making his act more and more dangerous, doing headstands, handstands, and toestands or hanging by one finger. Obviously, the risk is great, "but it's that kind of chance-taking that may lead to something perfectly amazing" (*Night Hurdling*). Of course, it may lead just as easily to something absurd, as it occasionally does, but that is part of the fascination, for the viewer as well as the performer.

His emphasis on reality notwithstanding, Dickey has never been one to court the quotidian. The routine of domestic life and the ordinary day-to-day task of walking through the world have never much interested him. That is why a poem like "The Hospital Window" ironically calls attention to itself, because it adheres to the commonplace. A man who has just visited his dying father in the hospital pauses in the middle of the street outside to wave to him and, with the traffic roaring all around him, waits for his wave to be returned. When his father waves back, the son takes it as a form of nonverbal communication, as a sign that the father is not afraid to die. Beginning and ending with the flat, unemotional statement, "I have just come down from my father," this poem draws as near to the straightforward, confessional style as Dickey gets.

Much more representative of Dickey's poetry overall is "The Sheep Child," which stands as a model for other Dickey poems. Its sensational topic, which provoked objection from some audiences in the 1960s, still has the power to unsettle the even more tolerant and "worldly" readers of the 1980s. Focusing on the offspring of a sexual encounter between a human and a sheep, the poem definitely has "presentational immediacy," if not

simple shock value. The sheep child speaks most of the poem from inside its
jar of alcohol in an Atlanta museum, a narrative strategy that has led Dickey
himself to say, half-jokingly, that he thinks the poem "can hardly be faulted
from the standpoint of originality of viewpoint" (*SI*).

But there is another speaker in the poem, a farm boy who has grown up
believing in the myth of the sheep child and who lures the reader into the
poem the way a good carnival barker pulls a crowd into the side show tent:

> I have heard tell
>
> That in a museum in Atlanta
> Way back in a corner somewhere
> There's this thing that's only half
> Sheep   like a woolly baby
> Pickled in alcohol   because
> Those things can't live   his eyes
> Are open   but you can't stand to look
> I heard from somebody who. . . .
>   (*Poems*)

By this point, readers are anxious to see this strange creature, and curiosity
acts as the force to pull them along into the poem just as it would carry them
past the gate and the tarpaulin flap at the county fair. The voice drawing
them in is that of the pitchman, confident and confidential, saying what the
farm boys say to "keep themselves off / Animals by legends of their own"
(*Poems*). The tone is that of the insider, of the one who has been there and
knows and cannot disbelieve the legend, wondering,

> Are we,
> Because we remember, remembered
> In the terrible dust of museums?
>   (*Poems*)

An irresistible momentum is created by the absence of end punctuation and
by the heavy enjambment in the first two stanzas, effects that contribute
greatly to the reader's involvement in the poem. An air of complicity, of
being party to an astonishing revelation, makes each of us as attentive as a
farm boy hearing the tale for the first time "In the hay-tunnel dark / And
dung of barns." The entire poem leading up to the sheep child's monologue
has a sotto voce quality, underscored by the repetition immediately before
the creature speaks:

> Merely with his eyes, the sheep-child may
> Be saying   saying
>
> *(Poems)*

This is vintage Dickey style, using repetition as a suspense builder, as an eerie fanfare to introduce the sheep child we've all been waiting to encounter. If the voice here sounds like the one used by children when telling ghost stories, the resemblance is no accident. In fact, the entire poem follows the ghost story pattern, complete with the unidentified source of information whose accuracy and veracity are implicitly beyond question: "I heard from somebody who. . . ." And when the sheep child finally talks, he speaks in the other-worldly voice appropriate to telepathic communication from within a bottle of formaldehyde. The sheep child's speech is set in italics, presumably to emphasize its eeriness even further.

What Dickey employs in "The Sheep Child" and in many other poems is a kind of folk narrative, story-telling characterized by its simplicity and straightforwardness. Because of its casual directness, "The Sheep Child" disarms and engages the reader with the immediacy of an oral presentation. Anyone within earshot would probably draw near to hear such a tale, just as most who start reading the poem find themselves swept along from line to line. Dickey intends to do more than startle; he uses the opportunity, after he has gained our attention, to explore one of his favorite themes—the relationship between the animal and human worlds. The sheep child is significant not as a grotesque mutation but as a privileged creature who *"saw for a blazing moment / The great grassy world from both sides"* (*Poems*). Having a complete understanding of both *"Man and beast in the round of their need,"* the creature possesses the kind of unified vision Dickey seeks throughout his work.

Except in those poems in which Dickey is self-hypnotized by the magical potential of the lyric, he avoids having what he once claimed to hate: a first line that "announces itself as 'poetry' " and "a special kind of poetry-language" (*Sorties*). In his strongest narrative poems, Dickey deliberately works against the blatantly poetic to make his poems accessible to the broadest possible audience. How he sets out to do this is described in the following journal excerpt from *Sorties*:

> What we need, as *our* breakthrough, is a poetry of extreme simplicity, where one thing is said per line; but that thing must have almost infinite reverberations. I am not talking about a gnomic sort of utterance, but some new, modern thing. The sources of language for this sort of poetry have hardly been

tapped at all. But if we can get this, poetry will have a great deal
more resonance for people who never read much poetry because
of the excesses of Berryman or the erudition of Empson. We need
to go a different way from that now. I suspect that narrative may
also have something to do with it, and if one could combine this
extreme simplicity of utterance with a great deal of penetration
and a narrative element of either an ultra-real or a surreal kind,
he would have what is going to be the wave of the future. Either
he would have it, or he would make it.

(Sorties)

These observations prescribe exactly the kind of poetry found in "The
Sheep Child." In his reference to Berryman and Empson, Dickey implicitly
sets up these two poets as representatives of the extreme camps of
confessionalism and formalism. His objective, however, is not to locate
himself somewhere on the plain between but to find entirely new ground. As
in "The Sheep Child," he wants poetry that is neither allusive nor confessional and that has a strong narrative component focusing on the "ultra-
real" or surreal. Of significance, too, is his emphasis on accessibility and
audience appeal. He wants poetry that sells itself to the reader.

Dickey's fascination with the surreal or the "ultra-real" introduces into
his work the Southern Gothic element found in the fiction of writers like
Eudora Welty and Flannery O'Connor. In his story of the sheep child,
Dickey uses Southern mythology much the same way Welty uses it in "The
Wide Net," in which a Loch Ness-like monster, rising from the river being
seined for someone presumed drowned, is proclaimed King of the Snakes.
Dickey's creature is as fantastic as Welty's and challenges credibility in
much the same way. Curiously, both Dickey's half-sheep, half-human ani-
mal and Welty's enormous serpent remain remotely believable; we want to
believe in them or cannot believe strongly enough in their impossibility.
Because of their mythic proportions, they stand outside life.

The Gothic, among other elements, makes Dickey a much more Southern writer than anyone, including Dickey himself, has acknowledged.
Though he has said, "It's important to me to be a Southerner" (*SI*), he has
qualified that assertion by insisting, "I would not under any circumstances
want to feel that I was limited in any way by being a Southerner, that I was
expected, say, by other people to indulge in the kind of regional chauvinism
that has sometimes been indulged in by Southern writers" (*Night Hurdling*).
Such loud objections to the regional label have obscured Dickey's true and
important kinship to the best writers of the South, particularly the fiction

writers. Far from indulging in "regional chauvinism," Dickey has adopted a narrative view that aligns him with those Southern writers who transcend their region by using it rather than ignoring it. Consequently, if the sheep child, looking out from its jar in the museum, reminds us of Enoch Emery's "new Jesus" in *Wise Blood,* an embalmed pygmy who also resides behind glass in a museum, the similarities reveal a shared perception of the bizarre and its mythic potential within the context of the South.

Another poem that calls to mind *Wise Blood* is "A Folk Singer of the Thirties," whose speaker, like O'Connor's Hazel Motes, finds himself preaching something he finally cannot believe. For Motes it is the Church Without Christ, but for Dickey's unnamed speaker it is the philosophy of capitalistic expansion. In both instances, the character attains vision after undergoing a physical ordeal. In Motes's case, true vision is received in the end only after he blinds and disfigures himself with lye; while Dickey's folksinger has a clear perception of America (a perception he later corrupts) through the spikes driven into his hands and feet as he rocks across the country after being nailed to the outside of a boxcar by railroad guards. The Gothic element, present in much of Dickey's poetry, functions just as it does in the works of fiction writers who have been labeled Southern.

Dickey finds in his folksinger a character who is also an adept pitchman. In fact, he resembles an evangelical preacher, especially in the following passage:

> One night, I addressed the A.A.,
> Almost singing,
> And in the fiery,
> Unconsummated desire
> For drink that arose around me
> From those mild-mannered men,
> I mentioned a place for a shoe store
> That I had seen near the yards
> As a blackened hulk with potential.
>
> A man rose up,
> Took a drink from a secret bottle,
> And hurried out of the room.
> A year later to the day
> He knelt at my feet
> In a silver suit of raw silk.
>
> *(Poems)*

Recalling a talk delivered in a Hooverville, in "a chapel of galvanized tin," the speaker is once again caught up in the evangelical mood. His personal anecdote reflects a stock device used by revivalists, the confidential telling of some story of success or misery to get the crowd emotionally charged. In this case, the folksinger's sermon is not about religious faith but about financial success, a special kind of American salvation as remote as heaven during the depressed thirties.

The A.A. sermon is only one part of a larger personal anecdote, the story of the speaker's enlightenment and subsequent disillusionment. The entire poem is a kind of sermon, although spoken from the folksinger's apartment. Waking "not buried in pebbles / Behind the tank car, / But in the glimmering steeple," the speaker finds himself transformed from the boxcar rider in touch with the power and potential of America to a kind of media preacher who has sold his vision for profit. The poem, then, is his confession that something has gone wrong.

Though "A Folk Singer of the Thirties" is weak in some respects, particularly in the way its ending pulls up short, its great strength lies in its narrative style. In the folksinger turned preacher, Dickey discovered a voice with considerable power, one that blends the lyrical talent of the singer with the preacher's gift for extemporaneous speaking. The result is a short-line poem with the compelling power of a song created as it is sung or a sermon delivered spontaneously.

As Thomas O. Sloan has noted, "Dickey has a deep sense of what speech, the spoken word, is." I would go further and say that Dickey, in all but his most recent poems, has been preoccupied with getting the spoken word onto the page without doing it too much damage. Of course, whenever speech is transformed into print it changes, but Dickey's special mission as a poet has been to discover ways to minimize those alterations. Whether in the casual, conversational style of poems like "The Performance" or in the more insistent diction of "A Folk Singer of the Thirties," his objective has been to escape the restrictions of "poetic" language, or to expand the boundaries of what may be considered poetic. This is the direction he sought, away from Berryman and Empson toward a "simplicity of utterance," and his search led him not only to the sermon-ballad but to other forms as well, including the pure sermon, third-person narratives, and dramatic structures that resemble transcriptions of dialogue.

The pure sermon is represented by "May Day Sermon to the Women of Gilmer County, Georgia, by a Woman Preacher Leaving the Baptist Church." Modestly understating the poem's dimensions, Dickey has called "May Day Sermon" "just a retelling of a local folk myth" (*SI*). The story that forms the text for the woman preacher's sermon is simple: a young woman kills her father and elopes with her lover after the father has cruelly beaten her for suspected sexual encounters with the young man. But such a brief plot summary fails to do justice either to the Gothic nature of the story itself or to the way the story is told; and the telling, in this poem, is everything. According to Dickey, what he hoped to capture in the narrative was language "which has a kind of unbridled frenzy about it, something like that frenzy found when a preacher—particularly of the rural, Baptist variety— works himself up into a state of fanatical, Biblical, unbridled frenzy" (SI).

Swept up in the spirit and emotion of telling the women of Gilmer County "to throw off the shackles of the Baptist religion and enter into an older world of springtime, pleasure, love and delight" (SI), the woman preacher attains the extreme height of religious fervor, as revealed in the following passage:

                        Listen   listen like females
        each year
    In May   O glory   to the sound   the sound of your
        man gone wild
    With love in the woods   let your nipples rise   and
        leave your feet
    To hear: This is when moths flutter in from the open,
        and Hell
    Fire of the oil lamp shrivels them   and it is said
    To her: said like the Lord's voice trying to find a way
    Outside the Bible   O sisters   O women and children
        who will be
    Women of Gilmer County   you farm girls and Ellijay
        cotton mill
    Girls, get up   each May Day   up in your socks   it
        is the father
    Sound   going on about God   making, a hundred feet
        down,
    The well beat its bucket like a gong.

                                                              (Poems)

The cadences of impassioned speech, with its repetitions—"Listen listen . . . to the sound   the sound"—and exhortations—"O sisters   O women"—place the readers in the congregation and invite them to be carried along on the pure flow of spontaneous language.

Though not alone in criticizing this poem, Paul Ramsey has made some of the most caustic remarks about it. Calling "May Day Sermon" a "very bad poem" resulting from "a failure in understanding the principles by which good or great long poems are possible," Ramsey invites a comparison of Dickey's poem and "The Eve of Saint Agnes," which he sees as similar to "May Day Sermon" in plot line but superior as poetry. The problem with Ramsey's view is that it fails, or refuses, to allow Dickey the latitude he requires. The Spenserian stanza used by Keats in his poem, whatever its qualities may be, is as far from what Dickey wants to do as grits are from tapioca. Consequently, if the poem fails according to the standards of the traditional long poem in English, that is because Dickey deliberately departs from tradition. The excesses and inconsistencies that trouble Ramsey and cause him to dislike "May Day Sermon" are natural elements of speech intensified by passion, not the flaws of a failed neoromantic narrative poem. Dickey is after reader involvement, not formalistic niceties.

On the page, the lines of "May Day Sermon" reach from margin to margin and are characterized by occasional gaps or spaces between words and phrases. The effect is not the same as that of prose, though the lines create a fairly dense block. In talking about this lining, Dickey has said, "I wanted to present the reader with solid and all but impenetrable walls—a wall of language in which you have these interstices of blank spaces at irregular places. It's a wall you can't get over, but you have to descend, climb down, in a way" (*Night Hurdling*). At the same time, the manner of presentation is intended to approximate the way the mind functions, sometimes hesitating, sometimes rushing forward. Overall, the poem has the appearance of a literal transcription of a sermon, with spaces inserted by the transcriber to denote pauses and associational shifts. Like most transcriptions of speech, this one is easier to follow if read aloud to reproduce, as much as possible, the quality of the original presentation. In fact, it seems reasonable to assert, as Thomas O. Sloan has done, that "the poem defies a silent perusal of its words on the printed page. It demands an oral reading." If this is so, then Dickey has attained the kind of "presentational immediacy" he desires in his work. By making the reader a participant in the poem to the extent of obligating him to read it aloud, Dickey has found the perfect way to retain the dynamic qualities of speech within the context of a printed poem.

"Falling," another long poem that has provoked a divided critical response, resembles "May Day Sermon": the page is dominated by the same long, split lines, and the language has the quality of extemporaneous speech. But here the narration is third person and the speaker has no clear identity. Consequently, the voice is disembodied and, probably, more poetic than

Dickey would have wished. Though the story of the airline stewardess is certainly dramatic, the poem lacks a dramatic context, like the sermon, within which the story can be presented. Thus, there is no obvious dynamic situation into which the reader can enter as complete participant. Even so, this poem also insists on an oral reading, especially because it is so fluid. With only ten end punctuation marks in the entire narrative, the story rushes or plummets toward its conclusion, just as the stewardess falls precipitously to her death. Yet this momentum can only be guessed at through a silent reading; it must be sensed through oral participation in order to be experienced and appreciated fully.

In "May Day Sermon," the myth of the young woman who murders her father and rides off on the risen ghostly roads of creeks with her lover is subordinate to the sermon within which it is presented. Its function is to help the woman preacher get across her message to the women of Gilmer County. In "Falling," however, the myth of the stewardess turned goddess in free-fall over Kansas is primary. Although the narrator stands between us and the stewardess's experience, he does not comment to any great extent on what her fall and her actions before impact might imply. We are left to find our own applications for the myth, and the process involves us even more deeply in the poem. Looked at side by side, these two poems represent variations on a single narrative experiment, as Dickey tests his open, speechlike forms in first- and third-person voices.

The same kind of experimentation is sustained in "The Fiend" and "The Eye-Beaters," each focusing on the psychology of a particular type of societal misfit. "The Fiend" employs a third-person narrative to describe the obsessed behavior of a homicidal Peeping Tom who watches from trees and bushes as women dress, undress, and go about their private lives. In form and point of view, this poem greatly resembles "Falling," and the split-line style is particularly well-suited to the psychotic personality under scrutiny. Similar in style, "The Eye-Beaters" is a curious mixture of third and first person, along with marginal summaries of the type found in some nineteenth-century novels. Under examination here are blind children who beat their eyes in order to "see" something—light, perhaps—but the speaker, imagining much more, fantasizes that they are able to attain a vision of prehistory, when the human race was young. Swinging back and forth between reason and invention, the speaker engages in a kind of internal dialogue, sometimes assessing things from the objective, reasoned distance of third-person, and sometimes being swept up in the subjectivity of first-person involvement.

Dickey seeks in all his split-line, open-form poems (with the exception of "The Shark's Parlor," which is a straight-forward first-person tale) an approximation of how the mind works. In "May Day Sermon," the mind is literally spoken, but in "Falling," "The Fiend," and "The Eye-Beaters" the story is internalized as an omniscient narrator delves into the conscious and unconscious minds of people under stress: a dying woman, a voyeur, and a visitor to a home for blind children (who happens also to be the narrator). In "Falling" and "The Fiend," the narrator comes between the poem's central character and the reader, eliminating the possibility of speech. But as the mixture of third and first person in "The Eye-Beaters" illustrates, Dickey is interested not only in speech projected outward but also in the kind of internal conversations we all experience, those running dialogues in which we ask ourselves, as if we were someone else, "Why did you do that?" or "What will you do now?" This is precisely the disembodied voice that inhabits "Falling" and whose detached but involved observations are ended by the first-person exclamation of the stewardess ("Ah God—") as she dies. It is the objective center in each of us that watches and, if called upon, could voice our secrets in its strangely distant yet intimate way, just as the voyeur's secrets are disclosed in "The Fiend."

All of this shows how fascinated Dickey has been with narrative technique as a device to involve the reader and thereby sell the poem. The fictional element in such narrative experimentation is strong, and so Dickey's poems often resemble stories. This is particularly true in poems that employ dialogue, "Mercy," for example:

> The girls that went up are coming
> Down, turning the leaves
> Of the sign-out book. You waiting for Fay? Yes.
> She'll be a little while. O.K.
> More ice, to ice-pack
> The gin. The last door opens.
> It is Fay.

Except for the odd spacing, Dickey's deliberate movement away from the split-line toward a poem balanced on the page, this could be prose, and so could the following passage from "Looking for the Buckhead Boys":

> Mr. Hamby, remember me?
>   God A'Mighty! Ain't you the
>   one
> Who fumbled the punt and lost the Russell game?
>   That's right.

How're them butter fingers?
Still butter, I say,
Still fumbling. But what about the rest of the team?
(*Motion*)

In these poems, Dickey has moved so far away from the lyrical that one feels compelled to ask if they are poems at all. The narrative element is everything, and some of the dialogue thumps as flat as bad prose. The danger in trying to reclaim some of the territory lost by poetry to the novel and short story is that one may take back too much and end up writing prose, which happens to Dickey on occasion.

At the outer extreme of Dickey's narrative experimentation and his dangerous attraction to the prosier aspects of fiction lies *The Zodiac*, the book-length rantings of a drunken Dutch poet, loosely framed within the comments of a third-person narrator. For fifty-three pages, the Dutchman hallucinates and rambles his way toward an understanding of the universe and his place in it. Dickey's admission that much of *The Zodiac* "is maundering, a lot of it is foolish and self-delusionary" (*Night Hurdling*) can be corroborated by almost any random passage:

You talk about *looking:* Would you look at *that*
Electric page! What the hell did I say? Did *I* say that?
You bastard, you. Why didn't you know that before?
Where the hell have you been with your *head*?
You and the paper should have known it, you and the ink:
you write
Everybody writes

With blackness. Night. Why has it taken you all this time?
All this travel, all those lives
You've fucked up?
(*Motion*)

Though other parts of *The Zodiac* manifest a bit more sensitivity to the sounds and nuances of words, there is absolutely nothing lyrical about this passage. The uninteresting language is matched by the banality of the idea it carries. The notion that black words on white paper are mystically symbolic is the kind of overblown connection that only a drunk (or perhaps a Byronic thirteen-year-old) would make.

Dickey claims to like *The Zodiac* because "it is such an unwell-made piece of work." Further, he says, "I think that if I haven't done anything else in *The Zodiac* I have truly keyed-in on one of the most important things in the relationship of a person to his own poetry—and that is the combination of foolishness, daring and self-delusion that is necessary to make memorable poetry" (*Night Hurdling*). His emphasis is not so much on the poem itself as on the attitude that made the poem possible in the first place; and he is saying that memorable poetry may yet be written, if *The Zodiac* should not succeed, simply because he possesses the necessary drive and bravado. In short, he is willing to take chances, to strike out in new and different directions "even if it's a long and costly mistake" (*Night Hurdling*). But while Dickey's courage may be admirable, some of its products are not. Still, the consummate pitchman has often obscured the distinction between nobility of effort and quality of product, so much so that a terribly flawed, adolescent poem like *The Zodiac* has been admired by some critics not because of the poet's accomplishment but because of his intent.

Most of Dickey's experimentation is aesthetically pure; it apparently proceeds from a genuine desire to break through to new, unexplored territory. But some of his efforts took a decidedly commercial turn in the 1970s as Dickey began literally selling his work, marketing poems as if he were working once more for the advertising firm of Burke Dowling Adams, which he left in 1961. Two such packaged poems appear in the 1970 volume *The Eye-Beaters, Blood, Victory, Madness, Buckhead and Mercy* but were first published in a popular magazine, *Life*. One of them, "Apollo" was written to commemorate the moon landing and is better than MacLeish's poem ("Voyage to the Moon") on the subject, though not so good as Auden's cynical view in "Moon Landing." Another, "In the Pocket," originally published as part of a National Football League section of *Life*, illustrates all that is bad about occasional poetry as Dickey has his quarterback speak these lines:

> Around me the wrong color
> Is looming   hands are coming
>   Up and over between
> My Arm and Number Three: throw it hit him in the middle
> Of his enemies   hit move scramble
>   Before death and the ground
> Come up   LEAP STAND KILL DIE STRIKE
>
>   Now.
>
> (*Motion*)

Such hyperbolic screaming must strike even the professional quarterbacks of the NFL as ridiculous. After all, football is only a game and, Dickey's assertions notwithstanding, not even a very apt metaphor for life. Moreover, one wonders how it is possible to leap then stand, kill then die, and still be able to strike.

Four other occasional poems appear in *The Strength of Fields* (1979), among them the title poem, which was read at Jimmy Carter's presidential inaugural celebration and, with its emphasis on kindness as the saving grace of humanity, stresses the simple virtues of humankind. Almost as effective is "Exchanges," delivered as the 1970 Phi Beta Kappa poem for Harvard University and not terribly dated despite its topical references to environmental pollution and the Apollo moon missions. Embarrassingly maudlin, however, is an elegy "For the Death of Lombardi"—not quite as bad as "In the Pocket" but almost—with its imagery of middle-aged beer guzzlers looking to Vince Lombardi as to Christ, who must surely rise and win. And trite beyond explanation is "For the Running of the New York City Marathon," which celebrates the event by dubbing every finisher a winner, a tedious tribute that must have been spoken at some point by every television sportscaster who has been given time on the air.

These half-dozen poems are worth noting not because of their quality, as should be obvious, but because they reveal the extent of Dickey's drive to sell the poem. It is possible that the level of Dickey's writing in a poem like "In the Pocket" was deliberately kept within reach of the broadest possible audience because Dickey wanted every television viewing football fan who might pick up a copy of the poem in *Life* to be able to comprehend it. But such mass marketing is bound to produce inferior poetry, regardless of its public relations value on the grand scale; the serious poet cannot long pursue the lowest-common-denominator style without selling his artistic soul in the bargain. At his best, Dickey has sold the poem through his serious pursuit of the narrative and his search for ways to involve the reader in the poetry. At his worst, he has lowered the standards of quality and sold a cheaper product.

NELSON HATHCOCK

The Predator, the Prey, and the Poet in Dickey's "Heaven of Animals"

James Dickey has been called a neo-Romantic primitive often enough for this appellation to have acquired a ring of truth, and the earlier poems in the volume *Poems 1957–1967* tend to bear it out. In the volume partially included there, called *Drowning With Others,* one of the concerns of a significant number of poems is with the kinship of human and animal, a phenomenon for which Dickey obviously has special feelings. For him the natural world is rarely a mere literary symbol of the "not me"; it is, rather, another chamber of the full life, one he is able to penetrate by means of the willful imaginative act. Essentially, it is in this all-embracing outlook that Dickey's particular Romanticism obtains.

Yet Dickey never fails to be contemporary, for all of his sanguinary urges to run with the beasts; as twentieth-century man he experiences the general dissolution and frustration that seem a portion of life in these times. I wish to point out how this feeling of separateness creeps in, and it will suggest a new meaning for one of Dickey's most discussed and most frequently anthologized poems, "The Heaven of Animals." In doing so, I must first briefly point out several other poems in which that imaginative bonding of man and beast does occur, and then show how "The Heaven of Animals" offers a counterpoint to them. In this difference lies, I believe, the key to that poem's significance.

"Listening to Foxhounds" dwells upon an instance of the speaker's almost furtive identification with a hunted animal. I say "furtive" because

From *Concerning Poetry* 18, nos. 1/2 (1985). © 1985 by Western Washington University.

Dickey substitutes the familiar "you" for "I"—although the voice is obviously that of a man within the poem's narrative frame. The speaker is a part of the magic circle of the hunters' campfire, "quietly sitting / With the men whose brothers are hounds." The distant hounds in pursuit set up a wailing, and the lead dog's baying is instantly recognizable to his master. At the sight of recognition in the face of the hunter whose dog has first raised the scent, the speaker imagines the eager hound at the other end of this telepathic connection:

> Miles away in the dark,
> His enchanted dog can sense
> How his features glow like a savior's,
>
> And begins to hunt
> In a frenzy of desperate pride.

The dog is enchanted not only by the scent, but by the bond that ties him to his master. Then, abruptly, the speaker considers the quarry, the red fox with whom no one seems to share any empathy. His rendering of the fox's maneuvers, however, tells us that at least one person present is feeling a brotherhood with the fox: "Who runs with the fox / Must sit here like his own image, / Giving nothing of himself." And if we, like the others around the fire, do not make the association, we can hardly avoid it when he continues: "And it is hard, / When the fox leaps into his burrow, / To keep that singing down." The poem concludes with the "secret" exposed, with the eyes of the others coming round to rest on "A face that does not shine / Back from itself/ . . . Like the face of the dead." We can almost see the invisible smile on that man's "secret features."

In "A Dog Sleeping on My Feet" a nearly identical theme is altered by a change in perspective, and the hunt becomes a metaphor of poetic creation. The speaker is infused with the dream of a hunting dog sleeping on his feet. As immobility kills the feeling in his legs, the dream takes over, moves up through them, "taking hold of the pen by [his] fingers." The poet becomes a medium, writing automatically "in a daze / The hynotized language of beasts." Soon the dog will arise and go out into the yard—the connection will be broken—and the poet's hand "shall falter, and fail / Back into the human tongue." The moment of creative fervor is transitory; the human tongue is inadequate. We do see here the imaginative life of the mind associated with the instinctive, irrational life of the beast.

The oddity about "Fog Envelops the Animals" is that while in the first stanza we are told, "Not one can be seen, and they live," there is hardly any further mention of the animals. The poem actually details a kind of death into nature of the hunter. The speaker becomes the embodiment of the ultimate predator—death—by leaving his "visible self" behind, by losing it in the fog, "the pale, risen ghosts of deep rivers":

> I shall enter this world like the dead,
> Floating through tree trunks on currents
> And streams of untouchable pureness
>
> That shines without thinking of light.

By forsaking human form for the invisibility of the fog, the man can "stand with all beasts in a cloud." His contact with the animals he hunts is pure, and in the sense that he now is a figure of death, he is perpetually among them, a part of the dampness, the scents, the mists, the trees: "Of them I am deadly aware, / And they not of me, in this life." The man is never as alive as when he becomes the white-hooded figure of death. The animals, though unseen, live, but the human must wait for his "long-hidden / Long sought invisibility" before partaking of that existence. The final stanza barely conceals a tone of positive relish:

> My arrows, keener than snowflakes,
> Are with me whenever I touch them.
> Above my head, the trees exchange their arms
> In the purest fear upon earth.
> Silence. Whiteness. Hunting.

(That first line calls to mind the hunters of "Heaven" with "teeth and claws grown perfect, / More deadly than they can believe.")

"A Screened Porch in the Country" consists of a common tableau, the rural family sitting in the glow of a screened porch surrounded by darkness, and, as Dickey tells us, "mainly nothing happens"—except that somewhere in that imaginary land between light and darkness, between hue and shadow, a connection takes place. The shadows of the family, cast into the yard by the bulb burning above them, are the natural extensions of their bodies. The animals who creep to the edge of the glow

> are floating beyond
> Themselves, in peace,
> Where they have laid down
> Their souls and not known it.

The shadow-world existence, in these moments of repose at the end of the day, is a part of the human family's rightful possessions ("In the midst of *its*

nightly creatures"), a part of them gained simply by sitting and allowing this
nightly communion to occur

> Where the people are lying,
> Emitted by their own house
> So humanly that they become
> More than human, and enter the place
> Of small, blindly singing things,
> Seeming to rejoice
> Perpetually, without effort,
> Without knowing why
> Or how they do it.

That "place / Of small, blindly singing things" again resembles Dickey's
"Heaven" where the animals come "beyond their knowing" in attitudes of
"acceptance, compliance."

Each of these poems—still more in *Drowning With Others* might be
cited—concern the interrelationship of man and beast, and each is in its way
an affirmation of the blessings to be conferred upon that man by the beast
in his nature. For Dickey, this effect is positive and can be seen in each of
these cases because in each the human being is present, either as speaker or
as observable subject, like the family in "A Screened Porch in the Country."
Now to move to the exception:

> Here they are. The soft eyes open.
> If they have lived in a wood
> It is a wood.
> If they have lived on plains
> It is grass rolling
> Under their feet forever.
>
> Having no souls, they have come,
> Anyway, beyond their knowing.
> Their instincts wholly bloom
> And they rise.
> The soft eyes open.
>
> To match them, the landscape flowers,
> Outdoing, desperately
> Outdoing what is required:
> The richest wood,
> The deepest field.

For some of these,
It could not be the place
It is, without blood.
These hunt, as they have done,
But with claws and teeth grown perfect,

More deadly than they can believe.
They stalk more silently,
And crouch on the limbs of trees,
And their descent
Upon the bright backs of their prey

May take years
In a sovereign floating of joy.
And those that are hunted
Know this as their life,
Their reward: to walk

Under such trees in full knowledge
Of what is in glory above them,
And to feel no fear,
But acceptance, compliance.
Fulfilling themselves without pain

At the cycle's center,
They tremble, they walk
Under the tree,
They fall, they are torn,
They rise, they walk again.

"The Heaven of Animals" is an oddly quiet poem even though the scene described could be characterized as one of Darwinian ruthlessness. The lines are mostly short—three-stress measures—steadily paced, and there is never any doubt that the unseen speaker is in absolute control of his utterance.

The location is more specifically realized in the first line by the immediacy of present time and place—"Here they are"—than by specific evocations. As we read on, we see the reason. This heaven is amorphous, with the existence of the animals themselves dictating its features after they have awakened from some previous life "in a wood" or "on plains." This place, if we can call it that, does share something with the human conception of heaven, for it is permanent, with "grass rolling / Under their feet forever."

With the second stanza, such similarities end, and the heaven of animals is apparently distinguished from any human ideal:

> Having no souls, they have come,
> Anyway, beyond their knowing.
> Their instincts wholly bloom
> And they rise.
> The soft eyes open.

These animals seem to have qualified for their rewards by virtue of a deficit—"having no souls." But this lack is compensated for by something else—their instincts which "wholly bloom." Here is a heaven uncomplicated by any questions of good or evil. No words of judgment have made it available, for that human factor does not exist. The beasts have simply become, somehow, more fully animal, their instincts honed and heightened. Reflecting the presence of these beings, the natural surroundings alter:

> To match them, the landscape flowers,
> Outdoing, desperately
> Outdoing what is required:
> The richest wood,
> The deepest field.

This heaven is figured in superlatives, a place where all is the same, only better, fuller, richer.

Then the poem shifts its focus and the next four stanzas introduce the animals themselves, but not through any particularized description. Rather, they are divided into two groups—the hunters and the hunted—and any world in which the inhabitants can be divided into two classes is basically uncomplicated. The predators are shown only to "hunt, as they have done, / But with teeth and claws grown perfect, / More deadly than they can believe." These are generic beasts of prey descending upon the backs of generic prey. It might even be argued that they are not real animals, but that is not important. The point that the poem seems to make here is that it is the act—what Paul Carroll calls "the ecstasy of violence"—which is most arresting. The lines which depict the slaying tell much about how the beasts are perceived through a man's eyes:

> And their descent
> Upon the bright backs of their prey
>
> May take years
> In a sovereign floating of joy.

In this image we can see the Disney nature film which [in *Self-Interviews*] Dickey claims provided a measure of inspiration for the poem, but we also are made aware of the timelessness of the vision. Like a film projected again and again, this same sacrifice in the jungle or on the veldt is a momentary stage in the natural cycle, certain to be relentlessly duplicated. Carroll explains the final word of the passage above in this way: "On earth, predatory beasts hunt only to find food; in heaven, they hunt only for the joy of it." This observation has some validity, as far as it goes, but I must disagree with Carroll's basic contention that we are seeing through the animals' eyes in this poem. The "joy" and "glory" of this heaven are imposed by the imagination of the man (or God, if you will) who has created this place. "Joy" and "glory" can only be perceived by the eye of the soul.

The second category of beast here, the hunted, reveals one more vital aspect of Dickey's creatures:

> And those that are hunted
> Know this as their life,
> Their reward: to walk
>
> Under such trees in full knowledge
> Of what is in glory above them,
> And to feel no fear,
> But acceptance, compliance.

In this world one's "life" equals his "reward," a truly Edenic state. Certainly, the awareness of one's place and the acceptance of it in the ever-shifting cycle of nature and history is a kind of perfection. The final stanza is a capsule of the entire poem, the Heraclitean cycle reproduced in miniature, serving also to end the piece where it began. The poem's structure reflects the cycle that is its ostensible subject.

But I must now return to a point made earlier and elaborate on it. It is a mistake to believe that the poet has intended us to see this vision of heaven through the "soft eyes" of its beastly citizens. The poem is a human utterance, "a man speaking to other men," and therefore the question of perspective and viewpoint is crucial. In this case it is the key to the meaning.

The questions that arise are, "Why has Dickey chosen to show us this heaven?" and further, "What does the poem show us about him?" Of course, we do not read poetry to learn about the lives of its writers; poems are a singularly unreliable source for such information. But we do read it to find out something more about ourselves, about Man with capital "M." So, let us say that what we have here is an unlocated, unspecific landscape with unnamed creatures in it, presented to us by an unknown man, not necessarily by our neo-Romantic-sportsman-warrior poet. What, then, is the consequence?

The poems discussed earlier all involve a human presence within the scenes or narratives, either in the form of the speaker himself or in that of people observed by the speaker, either an "I" or a "they" or both. We can assume again in "The Heaven of Animals" that a man is telling us of the heaven, but unlike the other poems, he is not in the scene which he describes, not strolling the "richest wood" or the "deepest field," but is somewhere else, excluded. (For a heaven of animals it is only appropriate that the sign above the gate reads—No Humans Allowed.) This exclusion creates the subliminal lament of the poem. Our speaker persists in observing, however, because he feels that something is here for him. In the chantlike cadence of his sentences and in the type of detail he dwells upon, there runs a current of wistful envy and longing. He envies the power of blood and claw—the elemental, instinctive act—a power made possible by the animals' curious lack of spirit.

Without souls, these beasts are spared necessarily the guilt, the desire, the fear, the frustrations that men know intimately each day. Each day we remark the mixed blessing of the soul, that complicating factor in our existence. The pure intellect would allow us to rationalize dispassionately, but the very nature of the soul makes that impossible; there is always more to consider. The events of our lives, if granted more than a passing glance, are never simple. At one time or another we have all envied the terrible bliss of a heaven like the one described, a submission to naturalistic urges. Dickey's choice of a preposition in his title is therefore significant. It is not "The Heaven *for* Animals" because the heaven is *for* the poet, for the man who considers it and creates it in his mind. It is made *of* animals living on the plane of instinctive motivation we humans have long since tried to bury or subdue. While this heaven is one into which the yaks and leopards and buffalo awaken, it is also a heaven from which we have awakened and found ourselves human.

At base a certain purity and simplicity are the attractions of this state, qualities which make possible the "glory" of the hunter and the "full knowledge" of the hunted with their "acceptance, compliance." These creatures are simple beings moving resistlessly toward simple fates "without pain," without fear. To live is their reward; they look no further and hope for no heaven. Not so for the man who stands by and watches. Dickey's demonstrated love for the primitive and elemental forces of the natural world qualifies him as one who would stand and watch. At the same time, his power as a poet guarantees us that only standing and watching would not be enough for him. "The Heaven of Animals" represents an instance of longing transfigured by creative power. This heaven is the poet's possession, a stay against the fear of death. In a strange way he has looked at the animals and, in so doing, confirmed his own fragile humanity as a man who cannot after all become a beast—in that respect he is like all of us—but he also realizes that there is a heaven there to be had, and in that sense he is like few of us indeed.

JAMES APPLEWHITE

Reflections on Puella

In considering the relation between these poems from the point of view of
a girl growing into a woman, and those poems of adventurous experience
from a masculine point of view which make up the bulk of the poet's work,
we should remember that the nature of the speaker, of his or her status in
the poem, has always been a crucial issue in the work of James Dickey.
Dickey helped resurrect the poetic persona from the crippling self-directed
irony of Modernism. His macho stance was not itself a problem except
insofar as it may have seemed to make Hemingwayesque claims reaching
outside the poems to a base in some grandiosely daring lifestyle. The point
lies in how often, from the beginning, Dickey avoided this danger, gave one
the impression of universal experiences encountered by a set of eyes and ears
and muscles representative of everyone capable of being excited by the
climb, the hunt, the stream. There was not so much the exposition of known
abilities and manly accomplishments, as of surprised discovery, as the
speaker of the poem encountered again a part of personality which had
already somehow fused with a like current in the surround of woodland or
war situation or crowded fairground. The excitement of Dickey has always
resided in how provisionally, at the outset, the poem's speaker has been
identified, how blindly and inevitably he has been called to by a deeper-lying
stratum of his being. Like Lear "he hath ever but slenderly known himself"
because the poet is in a sense all men (and all women), and thus knowledge
of the self can never be complete, must wait upon the compulsion outside

From *The Southern Review* 21, no. 1 (January 1985). © 1985 by James Applewhite.

the ego toward that energetic ground the poet shares with trout and his parents and all other riders on the crowded Ferris wheel and the fiend waiting in darkness in the tree.

Apollo is all light, technical means, sun-clarity, but the image of blindness haunts the Dickean universe, and the poetic transaction takes place often in darkness, even underwater. To find himself the poet must lose himself. "For I is another," said Rimbaud. Thus to take the identity of a woman (or girl) is only to enter more completely that voyage into the terra incognita the poet must always traverse in his "given" poems. If the daughter in "Root Light" in her numinous birth caul of bubbles is part of the quick heart of the river, then entering that other thing more completely would be to feel through her senses, wake in her psyche. This the poet has done in *Puella*. In a poem such as "Veer-Voices: Two Sisters under Crows" the author's single male identity is transformed, split, mirrored, and redoubled. One sister, the speaker, verges toward the identity of the other, and both represent the human tensions from "the night-mass of families . . . our stifled folk" as they are given tongue by the veering, dividing cries of crows. These alien voices, tight strung and barbed like the wire underneath them, fill the sisters' "surround," bisect it from all angles and make a multitongued "cry of unfathomable hordes," into which the sisters' tight unexpressed human individuality is fused and expressed.

In the face of the many problems caused in the West by the restrictive masculine sensibility, it is particularly interesting that now Dickey devotes a whole book to another point of view. Though I don't think it quite convincing to translate "The Surround" (originally published in the *Atlantic* as James Dickey's tribute to James Wright) into a Deborah-poem simply by the inclusion of a subtitle, that title itself *is* of interest: "Imagining Herself as the Environment, / She speaks to James Wright at Sundown." One part of the Hemingway persona tells of shooting the lion like a boast. It is not that aspect of the male self that *knows* the lion, feels from his arteries. That is a Hemingway (or Dickey) not locked in a uniform of male courage and will, but part of the hunting/hunted, terrified and terrifying frieze of animals and jungle. Part of the environment. If Dickey views this identification with the environment as feminine, then it is all the more appropriate that he take on the persona of Deborah, because at his best he is more among the animals than with the hunter; he is beyond any known identity, as simply the keenest edge of being alive in salt marsh or zoo, heartbeat and sinew.

Loss of self in the discovery of a more essential and continuous ground of perception is central to Romantic poetry. Keats thought of children just come into the world as atoms of perception, sparks of an original light of

seeing that was from God. Whitman in "There Was a Child Went Forth
Each Day" is delivered from knowing only the self of intentions, business,
willed projects by seeing the father as "self-sufficient, manly, mean, anger'd,
unjust"; the child's identification with him has been foiled by "the blow, the
quick loud word, the tight bargain, the crafty lure," and expands like a
spirit denied any single body to possess a partial residence in everything it
sees. In his sight of the "fish suspending themselves so curiously below
there" the word *curiously* reminds us of just how wonderfully strange are all
the not-selves becoming partial selves for the poet, as his never completed,
blind identity finds temporary home in mare's foal or old drunkard staggering home from the outhouse—as, for Dickey, in sheep child or in the
awakening of a girl/woman growing toward self-knowledge among crows
and cornfields.

Though *Puella* in its diversity (including, along with poems of nature
identification, others dealing with piano playing, dancing, and the art of
tapestry) resists simplification into a single developmental sequence, there is,
for me at least, a core of psychological process. Poems early on in the book
reveal Deborah waking to her individual identity, once with the aid of a
mirror ("Deborah, Moon, Mirror, Right Hand Rising"). This regarding of
the self by the self, in a circle shining with the moon, begins the relation
between the psyche and the world. But Dickey knows, and feels through
Deborah, the child's apocalyptic tendency to oppose this world (which
opposes its wishes), and has dramatized a holocaust of this location in time
and space in the initial poem: "Deborah Burning a Doll Made of House-
Wood." Yet the love of carpenters here, of their "God-balanced bubbles"
(in carpenters' levels) suggests an adaptation toward the structure of houses,
of adulthood, which is developing, along with the child's blazing ability to
negate the world about it, the "power to see / Pure loss." So as the sequence
moves on into later poems such as "Veer-Voices" a dialectic is entered
upon, and the psyche learns to express itself through identification with
things about it—as with these voices of crows. After poems of horseback
riding and first onset of menses, there is the lyrically mysterious "Ray-
Flowers." I am reminded of Blake's "The Book of Thel." The essential
metaphor of Dickey's poem is of a down-light drifting fall, and I suspect
that at bottom this fall is into the world we know, and *from* some center of
self-contained spiritual identity which still, as in the opening poem, opposes
the limiting holds of gravity and time. The image of a feather holds the
"whole mingling oversouling loom / Of this generation," and the persona,
probably now an adolescent, grows "Akin to it, down-haired, like the near
side of smoke." I take this to suggest a consoling poetic vision of lightness,

of potential imaginative flight, which helps compensate for "where we fall, or fell."

If my reading of "Ray-Flowers" as a poem of resistance to involvement with the physical facts, yet of final acceptance, is correct, then "Deborah as Scion," next, makes a great deal of sense. At the family cemetery Deborah sees her dead ancestors in a moment of vision. "Grave dirt exploding like powder / Into sunlit lace." From the "green mines" of the family plot, the lives and labor of these earlier women, their "dark dazzle of needles," are unearthed. Deborah, having discovered her single self in the world, having accepted this "fall," now feels pressing upon her the sequence of mothers before who have stamped her with their "eyebrows, / Breasts, breath and butt." She feels herself alive for a moment in their whalebone corsets, "closed bones" which suggest the body she has inherited as well as the restrictions of dress. These corsets are perhaps the epitome of confinement, the final indication of being trapped in a condition and a time. What I find hard to make sense of in the latter part of this two-section poem is the transition to a vision of whales and whaling. Are the whales, sounding and breaching, an image of sexuality? Is this a further compensatory freedom? I am not sure.

Dickey's tendency to use sensory illusion, (as when his father's hospital room keeps ascending toward "Heaven" with the momentum of an elevator ride in "The Hospital Window," *Drowning With Others*), seems related to his sense of awakening to the world and its curiousness. In "Heraldic: Deborah and Horse in Morning Forest" we get once again this immersion through motion in a phenomenal flux which is complexly, physically *present:* for the horse and rider, "twigs from all sprung angles" speed toward the eyeball, as these two race toward "the wildly hidden log prowling upward." World as process, as flow, as danger, seeks to engulf the perceiving identity. As when Wordsworth in book 1 of *The Prelude* sees the mountain rising through optical illusion to stride after him in his purloined rowboat, so the Dickean self feels Dionysian nature looming over in a tidal wave that threatens the small boat of ego and its limited capacity for identification. The confrontation is terrifying yet fruitful. If the poet or his persona rides out the surge, part of the blind world is given sight.

As "All Presences change into trees" ("Sleeping Out at Easter," *Into the Stone*), the one eye that opens slowly is the sun's, but also the poet's; and *"All dark is now no more"* because of his reawakened, world-creating consciousness. When the poet makes the rain "Take the shape of the tent and believe it" ("In the Mountain Tent," *Drowning With Others*), he is creating definitions, asserting order. These seeings, these comings back to the surface, counterpoint the blindnesses, the divings under. Dickey, like the paradigm of the poet as second Creator, is romantic, and therefore the balance may seem sometimes to incline more toward the flood than toward the Ark. But finally he is a poet who rides it out, whose reassertions of order evoke (and investigate) a crucial boundary: between the light of the farmhouse with screened porch and the dark with its nightly creatures, that the shadows of the figures on the porch stretch out toward. Like the poet, these figures in "A Screened Porch in the Country" (*Drowning With Others*) are extended into a world beyond the consciously human, there to be touched by the soft bodies usually repelled by the boundary of wire.

I can't help feeling Dickey is one of our most poignant literary enigmas. When we first met in the sixties, he the arm-waving windmill of energy, the eye of a hurricane of gossip and rumor, he sat quietly in my house for hours, watching the Masters on TV and holding my two-year-old daughter in his lap. Influenced, perhaps, by that memory, I have since felt an edge of delicacy in both man and poet that others apparently did not always feel. Now here in *Puella* the fight between warrior male psyche and "the enemy women" has been resolved in favor of a wider self capacious enough to include sensitivities that the aggressive personal identity may in some respects have offended. I see Dickey sometimes as a figure wandering a giant landscape, the hurt, lush South of our unconscious inheritance. The conscious, male poet, bearing his baggage of wound, prejudice, ego-limitation, is sometimes transfixed by magnetic lines arising from pasture, salt marsh, or Civil War battleground, to be made momentarily a voice expressive of the great life beyond him. "Birds speak, their voices beyond them" ("Sleeping Out at Easter"), just as the voice of the poet is beyond mere will, intention, personality of which a person might boast. The experiences which matter don't belong to anyone, man or woman. They are gifts to the species from its past, to the eye from its landscape. The anonymous, blind son reveals the light of the man's mind, of which he is father. Trees are resurrected from dawn mist within the eyes which create them. The historical personage and its burdens have been used by a larger self.

Not that any of this is easy or automatic. Dickey has devoted enormous labor to finding himself in his craft. It is just that he has had the final good fortune to lose that self in words as only the greatest have done: falling from a jet liner, undressing, or leaving the Baptist Church, a woman preacher, or here, now, waking to consciousness and womanhood as Deborah. We see in *Puella* that the powerful Dickey of old is still at work, and that he has succeeded in adding at least a handful of these new poems to the central canon. I am impressed by the singularity of taut, musical phrases, remembering Dickey the musician, composer of "Dueling Banjos" for the movie

Deliverance. The influence of Hopkins in these poems brings a tenser rhythmic and imagistic organization, pulls the rigging shipshape. At least "Deborah Burning a Doll Made of House-Wood," "Deborah, Moon, Mirror, Right Hand Rising," "Veer-Voices: Two Sisters under Crows," "Ray-Flowers," and the first section of "Deborah as Scion" will join the other great central Dickey poems we remember and reread.

Chronology

1923   James (Lafayette) Dickey is born on February 2 in Atlanta, Georgia.

1942   Attends Clemson College, South Carolina, where he excels in football, and Vanderbilt University, from which he graduates Phi Beta Kappa. He serves in the Air Force during both World War II and the Korean War.

1948   Dickey marries Maxine Syerson.

1950   Teaches at Rice University, Houston.

1952–54   Teaches at the University of Florida, Gainesville. In 1954, he is awarded a Fellowship from the *Sewanee Review*. He spends the year in France with his wife and two sons.

1955–61   Dickey works in advertising agencies in New York and Atlanta. In 1960, he publishes *Into the Stone and Other Poems*. In 1961, he abandons a successful business career to spend the year abroad on a Guggenheim Fellowship with his wife and two sons.

1962   *Drowning With Others.*

1962–64   Appointed poet-in-residence at Reed College in Portland, Oregon. In 1964 he publishes *Helmets* and *Two Poems of the Air.*

1964–68   Dickey is poet-in-residence at San Fernando Valley State College and, in 1966, at the University of Wisconsin at Madison. In 1965, he publishes *Buckdancer's Choice,* which wins the National Book Award in Poetry. In 1966, he begins a two-year appointment as Poetry Consultant to the Library of Congress. Publishes *Poems 1957–1967,* and *Babel to Byzantium,* a collection of criticism.

1969   Becomes professor of English and writer-in-residence at the University of South Carolina, Columbia.

1970   Dickey publishes *Self-Interviews,* an autobiographical work, a best-selling novel, *Deliverance,* and a book of poetry, *The Eye-Beaters, Blood, Victory, Madness, Buckhead and Mercy.*

1974   *Jericho: The South Beheld.*

1976   Dickey's wife Maxine dies and he marries Deborah Dodson. Publishes a book-length poem, *The Zodiac.*

1977   *God's Images.*

1979   *The Strength of Fields.*

1981   *The Eagle's Mile.*

1982   *Falling, May Day Sermon, and Other Poems; The Early Motion: Drowning With Others and Helmets;* and *Puella.*

1983   *Night Hurdling; False Youth: Four Seasons; For a Time and Place;* and *The Central Motion: Poems 1968–1979.*

Contributors

HAROLD BLOOM, Sterling Professor of the Humanities at Yale University, is the author of *The Anxiety of Influence, Poetry and Repression,* and many other volumes of literary criticism. His forthcoming study, *Freud: Transference and Authority,* attempts a full-scale reading of all Freud's major writings. A MacArthur Prize Fellow, he is general editor of five series of literary criticism published by Chelsea House. During 1987–88, he was appointed Charles Eliot Norton Professor of Poetry at Harvard University.

LAURENCE LIEBERMAN is the author of numerous books of poetry and a collection of essays, *Unassigned Frequencies: American Poetry in Review.*

RICHARD HOWARD is best known for his books of poems, *Untitled Subjects* and *Findings,* for his translations of Baudelaire, and for his capacious commentary upon contemporary American poetry, *Alone with America.*

PAUL RAMSEY is Alumni Distinguished Professor of English at the University of Tennessee at Chattanooga. He is the author of a critical study, *The Art of John Dryden,* and several volumes of poetry.

JOYCE CAROL OATES is the author of numerous books of poetry and fiction, including *Crossing the Border* and *The Wheel of Love.*

ROBERT PENN WARREN is the author of numerous books of fiction and poetry, including *Audubon: A Vision.* He is the recipient of three Pulitzer Prizes, two for his poetry and one for his 1946 novel, *All the King's Men.*

LINDA WAGNER is Professor of English at Michigan State University. She is the author and editor of numerous studies of contemporary literature.

NEAL BOWERS teaches English at Iowa State University, where he also directs the creative writing program. He is the author of a volume of poetry and a critical study, *Theodore Roethke: The Journey from I to Otherwise.*

NELSON HATHCOCK is writing a doctoral dissertation on Randall Jarrell at Pennsylvania State University.

JAMES APPLEWHITE is director of the Institute of the Arts at Duke University, where he also teaches. He is the author of several volumes of poetry and has received writing fellowships from the National Endowment for the Arts and the Guggenheim Foundation.

Bibliography

Algren, Nelson. "Tricky Dickey." *The Critic* 28 (1970): 77–79.

Armour, Robert. "*Deliverance:* Four Variations on the American Adam." *Literature Film Quarterly* 1 (1973): 280–85.

Arnett, David L. "An Interview with James Dickey." *Contemporary Literature* 16 (1975): 286–300.

Aronson, James. "*Self-Interviews.*" *Antioch Review* 30 (1970–71): 463–65.

Baker, Donald W. "The Poetry of James Dickey." *Poetry* 3 (1968): 400–401.

Balakian, Peter. "Poets of Empathy." *Literary Review: An International Journal of Contemporary Writing* 27, no. 1 (1983): 135–46.

Barnwell, W. C. "James Dickey on Yeats: An Interview." *The Southern Review* 13 (1977): 311–16.

Bartlett, Lee, and Hugh Witemeyer. "Ezra Pound and James Dickey: A Correspondence and a Kinship." *Paideuma* 11 (1982): 290–312.

Baugham, Ronald. "James Dickey's *The Eye-Beaters:* 'An Agonizing New Life.' " *South Carolina Review* 10, no. 2 (1978): 81–88.

———. "James Dickey's War Poetry: A 'Saved, Shaken Life.' " *South Carolina Review* 15, no. 2 (1983): 38–48.

Beaton, James J. "Dickey Down the River." In *The Modern American Novel and the Movies,* edited by Gerald Peary and Roger Shatzkin. New York: Ungar, 1978.

Beidler, Peter G. " 'The Pride of Thine Heart Hath Deceived Thee': Narrative Distortion in Dickey's *Deliverance.*" *South Carolina Review* 5, no. 1 (1972): 29–40.

Bennett, Ross. " 'The Firebombing': A Reappraisal." *American Literature* 52 (1980): 430–48.

Bly, Robert. "*Buckdancer's Choice.*" *The Sixties,* no. 9 (Spring 1967): 70–79.

———. "Prose vs. Poetry." *Choice* 2 (1962): 65–80.

———. "The Works of James Dickey." *The Sixties,* no. 7 (Winter 1964): 41–57.

Bobbitt, Joan. "Unnatural Order in the Poetry of James Dickey." *Concerning Poetry* 11, no. 2 (1978): 39–44.

Bornhouser, Fred. "Poetry by the Poem." *Virginia Quarterly Review* 40 (1965): 146–52.

Bowers, Neal. *James Dickey: The Poet as Pitchman.* Columbia, Mo.: University of Missouri Press, 1985.

Broyard, Anatole. "Dickey's Likes and Dislikes." *The New York Times,* 17 December 1971, 37.

Calhoun, Richard J. "After a Long Silence: James Dickey as South Carolina Writer." *South Carolina Review* 9, no. 1 (1976): 12–20.

Calhoun, Richard J., and Robert W. Hill. *James Dickey*. Boston: Twayne, 1983.

———, ed. *James Dickey: The Expansive Imagination; A Collection of Critical Essays*. Deland, Fla.: Everete-Edwards, 1973.

Carnes, Bruce. "Deliverance in James Dickey's 'On the Coosawatee' and *Deliverance*." *Notes on Contemporary Literature* 7, no. 2 (1977): 2–4.

Carroll, Paul. "James Dickey as Critic." *Chicago Review* 20, no. 3 (1968): 82–87.

———. *The Poem in Its Skin*. Chicago: Follett Publishing, 1968.

Cassidy, Jerry. "What the Poetry Editor of *Esquire* Is Like: Interview with James Dickey." *Writer's Digest* 54 (1974): 16–20.

Cassill, R. V. "The Most Dangerous Game of the Poet James Dickey." *South Carolina Review* 10, no. 2 (1978): 7–8.

Cassity, Turner. "Double Dutch." *Parnassus* 8, no. 2 (1980): 177–93.

Champlin, Charles. "Men against River—of Life?—in *Deliverance*." *Los Angeles Times*, 13 August 1972.

Clausen, Christopher. "Grecian Thoughts in Home Fields: Reflections on Southern Poetry." *The Georgia Review* 32 (1978): 283–305.

Corrington, John William. "James Dickey's *Poems 1957–1967*: A Personal Appraisal." *The Georgia Review* 22 (1968): 12–23.

Covel, Robert C. "Bibliography." *James Dickey Newsletter* 1, no. 1 (1984): 15–27.

Davis, Charles E. "The Wilderness Revisited: Irony in James Dickey's *Deliverance*." *Studies in American Fiction* 4 (1976): 223–30.

DeMott, Benjamin. "The 'More Life' School and James Dickey." *Saturday Review*, March 1970.

Dickey, James. *The Suspect in Poetry*. Madison, Minn.: Sixties Press, 1964.

———. *A Private Brickmanship*. Pasadena, Calif.: Castle Press, 1965.

———. *Spinning the Crystal Ball: Some Guesses at the Future of American Poetry*. Washington, D.C.: Library of Congress, 1967.

———. *Metaphor as Pure Adventure*. Washington, D.C.: Library of Congress, 1968.

———. *Babel to Byzantium: Poets and Poetry Now*. New York: Farrar Straus, 1968.

———. *Self-Interviews*, edited by Barbara Reiss and James Reiss. New York: Doubleday, 1970.

———. *Sorties*. New York: Doubleday, 1971.

Dickey, William. "Talking about What's Real." *The Hudson Review* 18 (1965–66): 613–17.

———. "The Thing Itself." *The Hudson Review* 19 (1966): 145–55.

Donald, David Herbert. "Promised Land or Paradise Lost: The South Beheld." *The Georgia Review* 29 (1975): 184–87.

Doughtie, Edward. "Art and Nature in *Deliverance*." *The Southern Review* 64 (1979): 167–80.

Eagleton, Terry. "New Poetry." *Stand* 12, no. 3 (1971): 68–70.

Edwards, C. Hines, Jr. "Dickey's *Deliverance*: The Owl and the Eye." *Critique: Studies in Modern Fiction* 15 (1973): 95–101.

Ely, Robert. "Rising and Overcoming: James Dickey's 'The Diver.'" *Notes on Modern American Literature* 2 (1978): Item 12.

Evans, Oliver. "University Influence on Poetry." *The Prairie Schooner* 35, no. 2 (1961): 179–80.

Eyster, Warren. "The Regional Novels." *The Sewanee Review* 79 (1971): 469–74.

Fraser, G. S. "The Magicians." *Partisan Review* 38 (1971–72): 469–78.

Galler, David. "Versions of Accident." *The Kenyon Review* 26 (1964): 581–84.

Goldstein, Laurence. " 'The End of All Our Exploring': The Moon Landing and Modern Poetry." *Michigan Quarterly Review* 18 (1979): 192–217.

Gray, Paul Edward. "New Fiction in Review." *Yale Review* 60 (1970): 101–8.

Greiner, Donald J. "The Harmony of Bestiality in James Dickey's *Deliverance*." *South Carolina Review* 5, no. 1 (1972): 43–49.

Guillory, Daniel L. "Myth and Meaning in James Dickey's *Deliverance*." *College English* 3 (1976): 56–62.

———. "Water Magic in the Poetry of James Dickey." *English Language Notes* 8, no. 2 (1970): 129–38.

Gunn, Thom. "Things, Voices, Minds." *Yale Review* 52 (1962): 129–38.

Heyen, William. "A Conversation with James Dickey." *The Southern Review* 9 (1973): 135–56.

Heylen, Romy. "*The Zodiac:* Hendrick Marsman, Adriaan Barnouw, James Dickey: A Case Study in Interliterary Communication." *Dispositio: Revista Hispanica de Semiotica Literaria* 7, nos. 19–21 (1982): 85–93.

Holley, Linda Tarte. "Design and Focus in James Dickey's *Deliverance*." *South Carolina Review* 70, no. 2 (1978): 90–98.

Howard, Richard. "Resurrection for a Little While." *The Nation,* 23 March 1970, 341–42.

Jameson, Frederic. "The Great American Hunter, or, Ideological Content in the Novel." *College English* 34 (1972): 180–97.

Kael, Pauline. "After Innocence." *The New Yorker,* October 1973, 113–18.

Kalstone, David. *"Sorties." New York Times Book Review* 23 January 1972, 6.

Landess, Thomas. "Traditional Criticism and the Poetry of James Dickey." *The Occasional Review* 3 (1975): 5–26.

Lensing, George. "The Neo-Romanticism of James Dickey." *South Carolina Review* 10, no. 2 (1978): 20–32.

Lieberman, Laurence. *Unassigned Frequencies: American Poetry in Review, 1964–77.* Urbana: University of Illinois, 1978.

Loftis, John E. "*Deliverance* and *Treasure Island*." *Notes on Contemporary Literature* 14, no. 4 (1984): 11–12.

Lukas, Cynthia K. "James Dickey's Ark." *Texas Review* 4, nos. 3–4 (1983): 49–56.

McGinnis, Wayne D. "Mysticism in the Poetry of James Dickey." *New Laurel Review* 5, nos. 1–2 (1975): 5–10.

Morris, Christopher. "Dark Nights of the Flesh: The Apotheosis of the Bestial in James Dickey's *The Zodiac*." *Concerning Poetry* 4, no. 4 (1982): 31–47.

Nemerov, Howard. "James Dickey." In *Reflexions on Poetry and Poetics*. New Brunswick, N.J.: Rutgers University Press, 1972.

Peters, Robert. "The Phenomenon of James Dickey, Currently." *Western Humanities Review* 34 (1980): 159–66.

Pierce, Constance. "Dickey's 'Adultery': A Ritual of Renewal." *Concerning Poetry* 9, no. 2 (1976): 67–69.

Shaw, Robert B. "Poets in Midstream." *Poetry* 118 (1971): 228–33.

Shecter, Harold. "The Eye and the Nerve: A Psychological Reading of James Dickey's *Deliverance*." In *Seasoned Authors for a New Season: Search for Standards in Popular Writing,* edited by Louis Filler. Bowling Green, Ohio: Bowling Green University Popular Press, 1980.

Silverstein, Norman. "James Dickey's Muscular Eschatology." *Salmagundi* 22–23 (1973): 258–68.

Simpson, Louis. "New Books of Poems." *Harper's Magazine,* August 1967, 89–91.

Skipp, Francis E. "James Dickey's *The Zodiac:* The Heart of the Matter." *Contemporary Poetry* 14 (1981): 1–10.

Smith, Raymond. "The Poetic Faith of James Dickey." *Modern Poetry Studies* 2 (1972): 259–72.

South Carolina Review. James Dickey Special Issue 10, no. 2 (April 1978).

Strong, Paul. "James Dickey's Arrow of Deliverance." *South Carolina Review* 11, no. 1 (1978): 108–16.

Sullivan, Rosemary. "*Surfacing* and *Deliverance*." *Canadian Literature* no. 67 (Winter 1976): 6–20.

Waggoner, Hyatt H. *American Poets: From the Puritans to the Present.* Boston: Houghton Mifflin, 1968.

Weigl, Bruce and T. R. Hummer, eds. *The Imagination as Glory: The Poetry of James Dickey.* Urbana: University of Illinois Press, 1984.

Williams, Harry. "*The Edge Is What I Have.*" *Theodore Roethke and After.* Lewisberg, Penn.: Bucknell University Press, 1977.

Wimsatt, Margaret. "*Self-Interviews.*" *Commonweal* 93 (February 1971): 501–3.

Winchell, Mark Royden. "The River Within: Primitivism in James Dickey's *Deliverance*." *West Virginia University Philological Papers* 23 (1977): 106–14.

Zweig, Paul. "The Strength of Fields." *New York Times Book Review,* 6 January 1980, 6.

Acknowledgments

"Introduction" (originally entitled "James Dickey: From 'The Other' Through the *Early Motion*") by Harold Bloom from *The Southern Review* 21, no. 1 (January 1985), © 1985 by Harold Bloom. Reprinted by permission.

"James Dickey: The Deepening of Being" by Laurence Lieberman from *The Achievement of James Dickey* by Laurence Lieberman, © 1968 by Laurence Lieberman. Reprinted by permission of the author and Scott, Foresman and Company. This essay later appeared in *Unassigned Frequencies: American Poetry in Review*, published by the University of Illinois Press in 1977.

" 'We Never Can Really Tell Whether Nature Condemns Us or Loves Us' " by Richard Howard from *Alone with America* by Richard Howard, © 1980 by Richard Howard. Reprinted by permission of the author and Atheneum Publishers.

"James Dickey: Meter and Structure" by Paul Ramsey from *James Dickey: The Expansive Imagination*, edited by Richard J. Calhoun, © 1973 by Richard J. Calhoun. Reprinted by permission of Everett/Edwards, Inc.

"Out of Stone, Into Flesh" (originally entitled "Out of Stone, Into Flesh: The Imagination of James Dickey") by Joyce Carol Oates from *New Heaven, New Earth: The Visionary Experience in Literature* by Joyce Carol Oates, © 1974 by Joyce Carol Oates. Reprinted by permission of the author and the Vanguard Press. This essay originally appeared in *Modern Poetry Studies* (Summer 1974).

"The Enunciation of Universality" (originally entitled "A Poem About the Ambition of Poetry") by Robert Penn Warren from *The New York Times Book Review* (November 14, 1976), © 1976 by the New York Times Company. Reprinted by permission.

"*Deliverance*: Initiation and Possibility" by Linda Wagner from *The South Carolina Review* 10, no. 2 (April 1978), © 1978 by Linda Wagner. Reprinted by permission of the author.

"Selling the Poem" by Neal Bowers from *James Dickey: The Poet as Pitchman* by Neal Bowers, © 1985 by the Curators of the University of Missouri. Reprinted by permission of the University of Missouri Press.

"The Predator, the Prey, and the Poet in Dickey's 'Heaven of Animals' " by Nelson Hathcock from *Concerning Poetry* 18, nos., 1/2 (1985), © 1985 by Western Washington University. Reprinted by permission.

"Reflections on *Puella*" by James Applewhite from *The Southern Review* 21, no. 1 (January 1985), © 1985 by James Applewhite. Reprinted by permission of the author.

Index